TO THE SNOWS OF TIBET THROUGH CHINA

THE AUTHOR IN CHINESE TRAVELLING DRESS.

TO THE SNOWS OF TIBET THROUGH CHINA

BY

A. E. PRATT, F.R.G.S.

GILL MEMORIALIST

1891

AUTHOR'S CHINESE NAME

WITH ILLUSTRATIONS AND A MAP

GYAN

Published by

GYAN

Gyan Publishing House
5, Ansari Road
Daryaganj, New Delhi-110002
Phone: 011-47034999, 9811692060
E-mail: books@gyanbooks.com

Distribution Network
gyanbooks.com
India, USA, Canada, UK, Australia, France

ISBN : 978-81-212-4123-6 (PB)
First Published, 1892

2nd Impression 2020

Printed at: Gyan Press, Delhi.

To the Snows of Tibet Through China
Author: A. E. Pratt, F.R.G.S.

TO

J. H. LEECH, Esq.

B.A., F.L.S., F.Z.S., F.R.G.S., &c.

A DISTINGUISHED ENTOMOLOGIST

THIS VOLUME IS GRATEFULLY DEDICATED

BY THE AUTHOR

PREFACE

It was not until after my return to Europe that the thought occurred to me of putting the notes of my experiences in China into the shape of a book, which is now presented to the reader. The work makes no pretension to be anything more than a straightforward, unvarnished account of trips into very little known parts of China and Tibet. I have avoided, as far as possible, descriptions of places and scenes which have been previously described, and have also done my best to withstand the temptation to generalise from limited experience, to which travellers in China seem peculiarly liable. I avail myself of this preface to express my deep obligations to many friends who have helped me in one way and another. Especially I would offer my thanks to Monseigneur Biet, of Ta-tsien-lu, for much kindness on the occasion of both my visits.

To Lieut. ALEXANDER COCHRAN, R.N., I also owe my thanks for his assistance in compiling this work from the rough notes of my journeys. Space will not permit me to do more than briefly express my thanks to the three following members of the Consular Service, Messrs. GREGORY, FRASER, and COCKBURN, late British Resident of Chung-king; also to the Rev. GEORGE COCKBURN and Dr. A. HENRY of Ichang, Bishop BENJAMIN, Pères SOULIÉ, DEJEAN, MOSSOT, and other fathers; Mr. THOMAS WOOD of Messrs. Drysdale, Ringer, & Co., Shanghai, the Rev. BENJAMIN RIRIE, the Rev. JOSHUA VALE of Kia-ting-fu, and the Rev. JOHN HYKES and Dr. UNDERWOOD of Kiu-kiang, from all of whom I received great courtesy, and all the help they could give me.

A. E. PRATT.

12 WINTON STREET, RYDE, ISLE OF WIGHT:
February 26, 1892

CONTENTS

CHAPTER I

THE YANG-TZE AS FAR AS ICHANG

CHAPTER II

ICHANG

CHAPTER III

EXPEDITIONS TO CHANG-YANG AND SIN-TAN RAPID

CHAPTER IV

CHANG-YANG

CHAPTER V

SHA-SHIH AND PA-CHOW

CHAPTER VI

THROUGH THE GORGES OF THE YANG-TZE

CHAPTER VII

JOURNEY UP THE RIVER CONTINUED

CHAPTER VIII

KIA-TING-FU TO WA-SHAN

CHAPTER IX

WA-SHAN TO TA-TSIEN-LU

CHAPTER X

TA-TSIEN-LU

CHAPTER XI

RETURN JOURNEY TO ICHANG

CHAPTER XII

SECOND JOURNEY TO TA-TSIEN-LU

CHAPTER XIII

TA-TSIEN-LU

CHAPTER XIV

MOUNT OMÊI

CHAPTER XV

OMÊI-SHAN TO SHANGHAI AND HOME

APPENDICES

ILLUSTRATIONS

TO THE SNOWS OF TIBET THROUGH CHINA

CHAPTER I

THE YANG-TZE AS FAR AS ICHANG

Object of journey—Departure from England—Arrival at Shanghai—Kiu-kiang—'Little Orphan'—Lu-shan Hills—Flowers—Temples—Rain-fall—New snake—Collector bitten—Silver work—Hankow—Passport obtained—Leave for Ichang—Sunday Island—House rented—Cess-pool—House-boat hired—San-yu-tung—Joss-house—New papilio—Ferns and plants—Fishermen—Birds and monkeys—Wild goats—Flying squirrel—Chinese mountaineers—General aspect of glen—Return to Ichang.

So little of this great world of ours is new to the explorer or the naturalist, that it becomes more difficult year by year to find unworked fields. Choice is therefore mainly confined to those which have hitherto been only superficially examined. The countries in which these occur are not easy for a European to work in, either from the hostility of the natives, or difficulty of travel and the transport of collections. After considerable thought I decided to proceed to China and ascend the Yang-tze-kiang, with the intention of penetrating Tibet from its eastern boundary. With this object in view I left England on February 7, 1887, in the s.s. *Palinurus*, bound for Shanghai, with my wife and family, who I intended should accompany me as far as Ichang, the last treaty port on the river. Nothing of any special interest occurred during the voyage, and as it has been frequently described, and is now so often taken by the ordinary globe-trotter, it will receive no notice in this work.

I arrived on April 2, and after a stay of a week, left in one of the splendid river steamers for Kiu-kiang on my way to Ichang, which place I purposed to make my head-quarters.

These boats are most luxuriously furnished, and the comfort of passengers is carefully provided for in every way. At Kiu-kiang my real work commenced. This town is situated on the right bank of the river, and just above the Poyang Lake. It is built as high as possible above the ordinary level of the river, but as violent floods occur during the summer, it suffers, like all the other towns on the flat banks of the river, from inundations, floods being caused by the melting of the snow on the mountains among which the river takes its rise.

Just before reaching Kiu-kiang one of the most

remarkable objects in the lower part of the river was passed—a huge isolated rock surmounted by a joss-house, which was embowered in gracefully growing vegetation consisting principally of bamboo. This rock goes by the name of 'The Little Orphan,' and it is worthy of note that pelicans are first met with here.

There being no hotel at Kiu-kiang, I was most hospitably entertained by Dr. Underwood till I could get away to the hilly country about nine miles to the south of the town, where I might expect to commence collecting. Here I got accommodation through the kindness of the Rev. John Hykes of the American Central China Mission. This gentleman most generously placed his bungalow at my disposal for the whole of the summer season. It was most delightfully situated in a gorge, with a beautiful view of the river and valley below. There were three rooms, with the usual verandah in front, and a detached cook-house. At the back was a precipitous hill covered with trees, scrub, and undergrowth. Numerous watercourses ran down, and after heavy rain the noise from the waterfalls was almost deafening.

These ranges are called the Lu-shan Hills, and the road from Kiu-kiang lies at first through a fertile valley in which rice is largely cultivated. About six miles out the ascent commences, and small streams passing through rocky ravines clothed with underwood are seen. Further up the vegetation increases in size, and consists on the northern slopes principally of coniferous plants and evergreens. On the southern side firs appeared to be more numerous than on the northern. Lilies of several species were common here. A few orchids were seen, all being terrestrial, and one species very fragrant. The wistaria grew luxuriantly, and its masses of lilac bloom formed in places a magnificent spectacle. White and yellow gardenias also grew wild in profusion. In these hills are several temples, and the trees around them are not permitted to be destroyed. This appears to be a universal custom throughout China. No great altitude is attained, but during the hot season they are much frequented by the Europeans from Kiu-kiang as a sanatorium, the natural pools being greatly appreciated for bathing purposes. There is a tremendous rainfall here during the months of May and June, but having no suitable instruments I was unable to determine it exactly.

Here I remained till August 4, all my time being fully occupied in collecting Lepidoptera and Coleoptera. Of the latter I amassed an enormous collection, among which were many new species, and of the former many were closely allied to the Japanese forms. I also made a collection of reptilia, among which was a fine new species of crotaline snake (*Halys acutus*). This was found at Wu-suih, about three days' journey from the bungalow, which place has now attained an unenviable notoriety for anti-European riots. Having completed my series of them, I refused to purchase another specimen from a Chinese collector, and he thereupon threw it among my children, who were in the verandah, with the charitable intention that one of them might be bitten. I am happy to say that his design was frustrated, as the poisonous reptile was promptly killed before it had time to do any harm. While here, one of my collectors was bitten on the thumb by a small red and black snake. His arm swelled very much, and on sending him to Kiu-kiang Dr. Underwood found it necessary to amputate his thumb. He resumed his work as soon as he was able, but one day had the misfortune to hit the still unhealed wound against a branch. This caused it to bleed so much that he with difficulty reached the bungalow, where he nearly fainted, and he had to be sent down a second time, in a chair, to Kiu-kiang for treatment.

In addition to forming these collections I had a large number of the larvæ and pupæ of Lepidoptera under observation, and found that procuring suitable food for the former occupied a good deal of time.

Near this place is a celebrated manufactory of china,

and it is here that all the Imperial ware is manufactured. It is hardly necessary to say anything about the town of Kiu-kiang, as it is a place comparatively well known to Europeans. The inhabitants are celebrated for their skill as silversmiths, and turn out much beautiful work which is highly prized by Europeans. During my stay I experienced much kindness at the hands of Mr. Wavell of the Imperial Chinese Customs.

On August 4 I left for Hankow and arrived on the 6th. The scenery ascending the river is flat and uninteresting, and nothing noteworthy was seen. Hankow is the great centre of the tea trade, and possesses the finest bund in China. As usual, however, as in most other towns on the Yang-tze, during floods the streets and bund are under water, and communication has to be made from house to house by sampans. I here obtained from H.M. Consul the necessary passport for the provinces of Hu-peh and Sze-chuen.

A delay of three days was caused by the steamers not running in connection with each other, and during this time Mr. and Mrs. Armour were most kind to Mrs. Pratt, my children, and myself. Had it not been for their hospitality we should have experienced great inconvenience from the mosquitoes and the heat. The s.s. *Kiang-tung* took us to Ichang, where we arrived on August 14. The river being now high, no difficulty was experienced in getting by Sunday Island, the channel past which is, during the winter and spring, when the river is at its lowest, always a cause of delay to the steamers. They always send a boat ahead to sound on the way up, and in spite of all precautions frequently get aground. The bed of the river here is very wide, and consequently shallow, and each year when the water falls low it cuts a new channel for itself. No permanent survey is therefore of any use, and the fairway is usually buoyed afresh as it shifts. This place is the most serious obstacle to navigation on the river below Ichang, and during winter, only steamers of the shallowest draught ever attempt the passage. This town is situated on the left bank of the Yang-tze, and 1,110 miles from its mouth. It is the last treaty port, and I considered that it would form a base for my work for at least a year. The first difficulty was to find a house for my wife and family, and this was by no means an easy task. It was, of course, impossible to live in the city, and for some time it appeared to be equally impossible to find any habitation near the European settlement. The Consul, however, most kindly lodged us for about a fortnight, at the expiration of which I was fortunate enough to be able to rent what was called a Chinese house. It really was nothing but an empty barn, with mud walls and a roof of timber and tiles. There was neither ceiling nor partitions, and the floor was of earth. Close to the side was a large cesspool that was replenished daily from the city, and in the evening its contents were used to fertilise a large garden opposite. The continual stirring of its contents made us quite aware of its fragrance, and though none of us suffered in consequence, my Chinese boy got typhoid fever, from which I am glad to say he eventually recovered.

We were not, luckily, obliged to stop in the house just mentioned during the whole of our stay in Ichang, for in September I hired a house-boat with six compartments, in which we embarked for the San-yu-tung Glen, which is situated on the left bank of the river, and just at the mouth of the Ichang Gorge. I fully determined to live in the boat as long as the weather would permit, and, leaving Ichang on the 10th, we arrived at our destination the same day. The boat was much more comfortable than the house in every way, and my intention was to make the most of the remainder of the season in collecting insects. I brought my Chinese boy up in the hope that the change would assist his recovery, and on arrival sent him up to a joss-house. He only was permitted to stay for five days, when his mother arrived and wished to make some of her 'joss pigeon' over him, and removed him for the

PONTOON, ICHANG.

purpose. He had, however, much benefited by the journey, and was nearly well when he left. The joss-house just mentioned is formed of a natural cave of great beauty and considerable size, the entrance to which is on the face of a precipice. Here I found growing in great luxuriance a variety of primula, the leaves of which are scented, and the flowers, which are borne singly, mauve. This grows in large masses and forms a most conspicuous object. The joss-house was certainly very damp inside, but was not considered to be unhealthy, and the chief priest has lived there for forty-five years, showing that it has not affected his health. It possesses a single bell of considerable, size, and the sound of its vibration and echo in the cave has a very weird effect.

We lived entirely in the boat, making daily excursions into the glen and collecting Lepidoptera and Coleoptera, of which I found a fair number. Among the more striking plants is the *bohenia*, which grows in great profusion over the rocks and bears very pretty bunches of waxy pink flowers. Lilies abound, and their flowers are eagerly sought for by the commoner papilios. Among them, however, I was fortunate enough to capture a magnificent new species, which has since been named *Papilio Elwesi.* Clematis and various species of fern abound, and in the more shady places a beautiful variety of begonia is found, which has white flowers with yellow centres. This grows principally in a bifurcation of the glen, called by the Europeans the Goat Glen. Maidenhair fern grows luxuriantly in the soft sandstone, and the Chinese cut large slabs, some of considerable size and weight, with the ferns attached, for sale to the Europeans at Ichang, from whence they find their way to the ports all down the river. Varieties of Daphne and Herb Paris are also found, and, on the hills surrounding, two species of persimmons (*Diospyros virginiana* and *D. kaki*) are grown in large quantities and exported. The whole place, and especially the Goat Glen, is very rich in vegetation, and Dr. A. Henry, of the Imperial Maritime Customs, a celebrated botanist, has found many new species here.

A stream of remarkably clear water having many tributary branches runs into the river from the valley, and fishermen may be seen using the casting-net with great skill near the mouth. Further up, where the water is shallower, they capture fish by the method known in this country as 'tickling.' Water ouzels are common, and high up the stream among the precipices I saw a large species of grey kingfisher which nests in holes in the cliffs. It is, however, by no means common, and I failed to procure a specimen. A few monkeys are to be seen, but they appeared to be very shy.

PAPILIO ELWESI.

The Goat Glen mentioned before is a branch of the San-yu-tung, and is so called from its being inhabited by a species of wild goat. Owing to the wildness and precipitous nature of the locality, it seems to be particularly adapted to their habits.

Picture to yourself a deep valley, with the entrance very narrow and steep, widening out here and there into broad cup-shaped expansions almost surrounded by unscalable precipices, and here and there huge piles of enormous boulders lying in the greatest confusion, a small stream of water running through the centre fed by several rivulets, plants of almost innumerable species, many being of great beauty, growing in every possible place, and some idea may be formed of this exquisite gorge.

It may be imagined that in such a place it is not easy to get a shot at the goats, particularly as they conceal themselves in the luxuriant vegetation for the greater part of the day. The most practicable way is for the sportsman to gain the summit of the cliff in such a place as to command a view of the valley in one of its wider parts, taking care to get there as quietly as possible.

The beaters also ascend, but on the opposite side, and hurl huge stones over the precipice. These descend by leaps of hundreds of feet into the valley beneath, and startle the goats from their concealment, when they invariably make for the higher ground, and being then more exposed, frequently offer a good shot. I am doubtful as to the species of these goats, but a fine living adult specimen has been obtained, and is now, I believe, in the possession of Père Heurde, in his garden at Sicawei.

A beautiful flying squirrel is also found here. One was obtained alive by Percy Montgomery, Esq., of the Imperial Maritime Customs, and sent by him to the gardens of the Royal Zoological Society, where it is still living.

The hill Chinese are exceedingly good mountaineers, and it is most alarming to see them on the face of a cliff nearly perpendicular, finding foothold on ledges only a few inches wide, with a sheer drop of perhaps hundreds of feet beneath them. If a break occurs in the ledge, and there should happen to be any vegetation over their heads, they will not hesitate to seize it with their hands and swing themselves over the gap. It is a thing to be seen before one can thoroughly comprehend it, and I heard, without much surprise, that loss of life by accident was not unfrequent among them.

The whole aspect of these gorges is beautiful in the extreme. Lofty precipices, clear limpid streams, luxuriant vegetation, and charming flowers combine to make it one of the most delightful spots I have ever visited, and it was also the furthest point from civilisation I had as yet reached on this journey. The increasing cold, however, and the scarcity of specimens for collection, warned me of the advanced season, and in the beginning of October I reluctantly decided to return to Ichang.

CHAPTER II

ICHANG

Packing collections—Packing-cases—Curiosities—Trade of Ichang—Imports—Communication with Hankow—Missions and missionaries—Festival of New Year—Beggars, their misery and harsh treatment—Procession to pray for rain—Joss-house to bring luck—Golden pheasants—Fish of the Yang-tze—River porpoise—Otters for fishing—Cemetery—The Dome—Floating lamps.

ON my return to Ichang I at once set about putting my collections in order, with the view of sending them home at the earliest opportunity for classification. This, of course, took considerable time, not in the arranging and the packing alone, but in seeing that in the first place the tin linings of the cases were perfectly air-tight. Many of them were made in Shanghai, and I always tested them by filling with water, when the slightest fault could be detected. Having been thus tried, they were emptied and thoroughly dried. The upper edges of the tin were flanged inwards, and then when the case was carefully packed a sheet of tin was laid on the flanges and carefully soldered down, taking especial care that the corners were particularly examined, as this was found to be the most difficult part in which to make a perfectly tight join. The Chinese are excellent workmen, and could do all this work very well indeed when they liked, but I found that they required continual watching, otherwise they were apt to scamp the work. They could not understand, either, the value I set on my collections, and therefore did not see the necessity for all the care I insisted upon having bestowed on them.

Many objects of great curiosity are found in Ichang, and are much valued by the Chinese as well as by the Europeans. Among them may be mentioned a very hard and dense black stone, in which iron pyrites occurs in lumps of irregular sizes and shapes. These stones are beautifully decorated in relief with human figures, animals, or plants, the pyrites being most cleverly brought in as eyes, ornaments, fruits, or flowers. The largest that I saw might be about thirty inches by twenty-four, and they are executed in many smaller sizes. The stone itself resembles compact lava, but I am unable to say what it is.

Another curiosity is what is called the pagoda stone, and is a species of belemnite with concave sections. They are nearly always brought in as sections cut in the natural block of stone in which they occur. This stone being of a dark colour and the fossil that is embedded in it white, or nearly so, and sometimes as much as thirty inches in length, they have when perfect and polished a very handsome appearance. Very powerful bows may be purchased here, and I brought home two, as well as some arrows. They are carried by some of the Chinese soldiery in the district, who are very well skilled in their use.

As the weather was now much cooler than when I first arrived, I found it more pleasant to explore the city, which is walled, and with, as usual, very narrow streets. It is comparatively clean to some Chinese towns I have been in, and contains about 70,000 inhabitants.

There is a large guild (called the Sze-chuen guild) on the bank of the river, and this is of considerable importance to the town. It is, of course, entirely for the up-river trade, and as the character of the river here changes completely (the banks instead of being flat become precipitous, for the mountainous region is nearly now reached), the navigation becomes much more difficult. The Hankow boatmen, indeed, refuse to proceed further, and if the same boat is to continue to ascend she must have another crew. The greater part of the population is engaged in the transport of goods in one way or another, there being a very large export as well as import trade. Of the exports, the principal are medicines brought down from Sze-chuen and Tibet;

these consist largely of rhubarb, of which a great quantity goes to Europe, and the remainder of elk horns, dried centipedes, *pey-mou*, and *Tchöng-Tsüo*. All these latter are used exclusively by the Chinese, and the last-named is a most curious plant, growing at a great elevation in the eastern part of Tibet. It has a single spathe-shaped leaf about three inches long, and the root bears the most extraordinary resemblance to a caterpillar, all the segments, legs, eyes, &c. being faithfully represented.

Large quantities of raw silk also pass through on the way to Shanghai, and a considerable quantity of musk.

There is a large import trade of Manchester goods, cotton, long-cloth, figured prints, and velveteen. These arrive in bulky bales, and are here examined by the Custom House officials. They are then made up in smaller packages more suitable for the up-country transport. Quicksilver is also imported in heavy iron bottles for use in the silver mines of Yunnan. There is a fine new China merchants' 'go-down' where all these articles may be seen.

The time of arrival of a steamer from Hankow is, in the winter and spring, when the river is low, very uncertain, the navigation being difficult owing to the channels constantly changing, more particularly at

Sunday Island, about halfway between the two places. In the summer and autumn there is plenty of water. The arrival of a steamer is always an exciting event to the Europeans.

There is only one Protestant mission here—that of the Church of Scotland—and it is in charge of a most zealous missionary, the Rev. G. Cockburn, who is the oldest European inhabitant and a first-rate Chinese scholar. He is greatly assisted in his many and varied duties by his wife, who was the first European lady to ascend the river beyond Hankow.

They reside in a small bungalow, which is made a frequent house of call by Protestant missionaries of all denominations and travellers passing up and down the river, who have all to be thankful for the hospitality of these kind-hearted people.

The Roman Catholics have also a mission, presided over by Bishop Benjamin, whose predecessor died of cholera shortly after my arrival. This disease works great havoc at certain seasons among the natives. The Rev. Father kindly gave me useful letters of introduction to the missionaries further west. He has recently erected a fine building facing the river, into which the Franciscan Fathers have been transferred, their old mission house being now inhabited by the Sisters who have lately arrived. While the new building was in course of construction, he suffered a severe loss in the almost total destruction by fire of an immense mass of timber which was to be used for it. On the alarm being given all the Europeans turned out to his assistance, but, owing to the want of any efficient fire-engine, were unable to be of much use. After a considerable time a mandarin appeared with several European portable hand fire-engines, but the small jets of water thrown by them were of no avail to extinguish the now fiercely burning pile.

On proceeding to the scene of the conflagration, I was somewhat surprised to find a Chinaman at a considerable distance from it diligently throwing water upon the reflection of the flames on the eaves of his house. Finding it impossible to satisfy him that his house was not on fire, I left him to his unprofitable labour.

In 1888 the Chinese new year occurred about the middle of February, and this is the most important festival in the year. During the ceremonies all work is suspended, and the whole population give themselves up to festivity and the payment of new year calls. All monetary settlements are concluded, and should a Chinese find himself unable to meet his liabilities, he frequently prefers death by his own hand to the dishonour. At this season it is the custom to send a servant to paste the card of the intending visitor upon the doors of all his acquaintances, and the effect of the doors sometimes almost covered with visiting cards of various colours is rather curious. I do not know whether this custom is general.

When the river is low, in the winter and early spring, numbers of beggars may be seen inhabiting the shallow caves scooped out by the action of the water on the bank, which is composed of conglomerate.

Here they exist—for it can hardly be called living—in a most miserable state, skinning and cooking for food cats, dogs, or anything that they can lay their hands upon, totally indifferent as to whether they have caught and killed them or whether they have died a natural death, many lying upon small heaps of damp straw or reeds, and all in such a state of disease, dirt, and destitution as would be hardly credited. When in the town the beggars all carry sticks to protect themselves from the dogs, who instinctively seem to know and invariably attack them on leaving a house where they have been begging. These beggars are very persistent, but are sometimes cruelly treated by their richer brethren. A case came to my knowledge where a rich Chinese caused a quantity of boiling water mixed with wood ashes to be thrown over the back of one who had seated himself on his doorstep and refused to leave. The unfortunate man, who was terribly injured, was taken to the Rev. G. Cockburn's hospital for treatment, where his wounds were dressed, but they were so severe that he died in a few days. No one was punished for this, the mandarin declining to take any action in the case as the injured man's friends had no money and, therefore, he could not squeeze them.

In February the ground was covered with snow, the river very low, and looking as black as ink. It was difficult to realise that in August the heat had been so intense.

Various kinds of vegetables are grown in the vicinity of the town, also cotton; and women may be seen spinning and weaving the latter into yarn and cloth while sitting outside the doors of their houses.

In times of unusual drought long processions headed by a magistrate may be seen. The men composing them are decorated with wreaths of small green branches of trees intermingled with lotus leaves, and many carry gongs or brass cymbals, as considerable noise seems to be considered necessary to attract the deity's attention. Thus they perambulate the town and the droughty fields until the rain comes, which is then attributed to their efforts or entreaties.

On the opposite side of the river to the English settlement there is a conspicuous pyramidal hill. For some reason or another the natives took it into their heads that this would bring luck to the foreigners, and they therefore, at considerable expense, built a joss-house on a hill of nearly as great an altitude, situated about a mile from the town at the back of the settlement (taking care that the top of the joss-house should be higher than the top of the hill on the other side of the river), in order to transfer the good luck to their city. From this joss-house a beautiful view of the city, settlement, and surrounding country is obtained.

Numbers of Golden Pheasants can be purchased in the autumn. They are brought to market in cages much too small for them, and in consequence their plumage is greatly damaged. As I wished to keep some till they had moulted and attained their full beauty, I had an aviary built, into which, when completed, I turned about fifteen couple, which I had bought at the cost of about 400 cash, or say two shillings, the pair. A heavy fall of snow unfortunately broke the roof in and many escaped, the remainder being killed by stoats, which are very numerous and exceedingly audacious. No place appeared safe from them, for they would steal chickens frequently from the house, and even if my boat was alongside the bank with the gangboard out, would come on board to forage.

A large species of sturgeon, *Psephurus gladius*, may be seen exposed for sale in sections in the city, the flesh much resembling beef in appearance. These fish sometimes attain a weight of over 2,000 lbs., and are captured in nets. The meat is, however, coarse and unpalatable to Europeans. When on an expedition down the river I once had an opportunity of purchasing a living specimen; but though I was only about eighty miles from the town, the fisherman refused to take my Ichang notes, which was the only form of money I had with me; consequently this chance of securing a large specimen to send home was lost.

An excellent fish for food, and much appreciated by the Europeans, is the mandarin fish. It is small and averages about a pound, rarely reaching more than four, in weight. Shaped somewhat like a bream, it is of a beautiful light silvery brown colour on the back and silvery white underneath. It is fairly common, and is captured both by nets and lines. In the river is also found a large species of carp, which forms a considerable article of diet among the natives; it attains a weight of 25 lbs. The whole river is teeming with fish of many other sorts, which are much fished for by the natives, who are expert anglers, in various ways.

The abundance of fish is so great that the natives are at certain times in the habit of setting long lines with many hooks attached to short lengths at small intervals. These are shot across the stream without any bait whatever, and with a bamboo buoy, in which there is a bell, at the further end. The fish coming down the stream are caught in quantities (hooked foul, of course), and if one of special size is hooked, its struggles set the bell in the buoy ringing, and the boatmen proceed out to secure it. Sometimes they have the misfortune to lose the whole line through the hooking of a fresh-water cetacean which inhabits the river, and which is much too strong for such gear as they use.

This river porpoise grows to a weight of about 1,000 lbs., so that it was useless to think of trying to send a full-grown specimen home. After some little trouble I procured one of about 150 lbs., and even then had great difficulty in finding a vessel large enough to contain it. At last I got a wine cask from the Franciscan Brothers, and half filling it with the native spirit called *samshew*, distilled from Indian corn, placed him in it with my other collection of fishes, then heading the cask up and filling with spirits, it was consigned home, and, I am glad to say, reached there safely.

Situated on the opposite bank of the river to the town is a small village, known to the Europeans as the 'Otter Village,' from the fact that the natives there make use of otters for fishing. These otters may be seen any day tied up in the bows of the sampans, and appear to be quite tame.

On the other side of the river, at the village of Annan-miao, the Europeans have a small cemetery, where they have great difficulty in preventing the Chinese from desecrating the graves. During my stay I was present at the funeral of a young missionary who had died of dysentery at Sha-shih.

An interesting trip may be made from Ichang to a hill known to Europeans as 'The Dome.' It is situated some little distance inland on the right bank of the river below the town, from which it may be seen on clear days, the top of the hill having a dome-like appearance, whence its name. It is approached by a very picturesque valley, which is called the Monastery Valley, in which there is a temple and cave, called Lung-woung-tung, on the side of a hill. In the cave is a lake which is held in great veneration by the Chinese, and which has no visible inlet or outlet. Europeans are not allowed to thoroughly explore it, and it is probable that it is some enlargement of a subterranean river, which are not uncommon in the district.

In the month of September one is often surprised to see thousands of tiny lighted lamps floating down on the surface of the river. They sometimes extend for miles, and are started at some little distance above the Chinese city. They are offerings to the deity for the souls of those who have lost their lives by drowning in the river, and consist simply of a cup with a little oil, into which a wick extends. The wicks are formed of the pith of a rush which is found higher up the river, the trade in which is considerable and the mode of transport curious. Several boats being lashed together, huge stacks of the pith, packed in bales, are built upon them until the structure is the size of a good large house. They are then floated down the stream, and the wonder of a stranger on first seeing such a floating pile is exercised as to what it can possibly be.

The illustration is taken from a photograph of Ichang when the river was low. The flagstaff shows the position of the British Consulate, to the left is the Chinese city, and in front are to be seen the caves mentioned in this chapter, in which the beggars make their dwelling.

ICHANG, SHOWING BRITISH CONSULATE.

CHAPTER III

EXPEDITIONS TO CHANG-YANG AND SIN-TAN RAPID

Want of forest near river—Chang-yang—Journey to—Description of Country—Pigs and leopards—Jungle—Reeves' pheasant—Return to Ichang—Enormous creepers—Soap trees—Ichang Gorge—Pin-san-pa—Mu-tan Rapid—Ta-tung Rapid—Curiously worn rocks—Crews of large junks—Lu-kan Gorge—Shale—Sin-tan Rapid—Me-tan Gorge—Insults at Sin-tan—Chinese monopoly of steam navigation—Steps up precipices—Nan-too—'Needle of Heaven'—Arrival at Ichang.

THE chief difficulty that presents itself in China to the entomologist is the lack of accessible virgin forest, and the want of reliable information as to where the rarer, or perhaps as yet undiscovered species, may be expected to be found. The rivers appear to be the natural high-roads of the natives, and as the banks are generally thickly populated, the forest has long ago disappeared. Marco Polo spoke of the river Yang-tze as being thickly wooded in places where a tree is not now to be seen for miles, and at the present day there are no trees worth felling within any distance of a stream that might be utilised to float the logs to a market.

After many inquiries, I heard from a native botanical collector in the employ of Dr. Henry that a district such as I was in search of might be found at three days' journey south of Ichang, in the district of Chang-yang, where the forest was of considerable extent, and where also he had a house. I therefore determined to make an expedition to see if the country bore out his description, and accordingly set out on the morning of October 7, 1887, with three coolies and a cook, who also acted as interpreter. My journey was made partly on foot and partly in a chair. After crossing the river and traversing the flat country on the banks I entered a valley, and found my first sleeping station on a small hill called Shih-te-yah, twenty miles from the start. Here I found the country beginning to get interesting to a naturalist. On starting the next morning I found the road at first descended slightly, and now the pine trees appeared growing in clumps in a soil of a rufous-brown colour. These were the first coniferous trees met with, and I now entered a valley of great beauty, which was studded with precipitous knolls crowned with a few firs and thick undergrowth. This valley trends to the westward for seven miles, and one passes through shady copses of graceful bamboo, some being nearly a mile long. As I proceeded the vegetation became much more varied, and patches of cultivated ground were met with. It had every appearance of being rich in entomological species, and I determined to make a station here at the proper season the following year for the purpose of collecting. After proceeding for about seven miles further I came to some paper mills, where the material manufactured is bamboo. The buildings, or rather huts, were wretched in the extreme, but as there was no choice of better, I decided to stop the night. Starting at 7.30 A.M. the next day, the first range of hills was soon met with. The road turned sharply to the left and led nearly due south, the ascent being very steep in some places; so much so, indeed, that in many places flights of steps had been cut.

I passed many beautiful gorges and valleys, and having travelled about fifteen miles over a very up-and-down road, reached a small Chinese village of about 250 huts, but which contained a new native inn, where I took up my quarters, and found it, for a wonder, to be very clean. The highest altitude reached during the day was nearly 3,000 feet, and the village was situated in a valley.

The next morning, after journeying for an hour along the ordinary road, I arrived at the foot of a high range, which I called afterwards the 'barrier.' I here determined to leave the main road and make the ascent; but as it was exceedingly steep and precipitous, and the mountain foot-trail very rough and winding, it was necessary to get additional assistance in carrying the loads, the Ichang coolies being quite incapable of getting them up; and luckily I was able to engage some of the mountaineers, who have a totally different way of carrying from the natives of the plains. They have a deep conical basket, flattened on the side which is next their back, and springing round in a bold semicircle. At the top of the flat side are two large beckets through which the arms are passed. This is called a *pey-dza*, and after it has been filled to the brim they pile up articles on the top till they reach high above their heads when in the carrying position, and lash them securely down. They all carry sticks, and use them when resting to support their loads, one end being placed on the ground and the other under the bottom of the *pey-dza*.

The ascent took about two hours and a half, and there was only one hut on the path up. Here, the owner being luckily at home, we were able to get some water and rest awhile. From this point the track trends to the west and is more level, and at about midday I arrived at two huts. The aneroid here showed that the altitude reached was 4,200 feet. The country was park-like, with detached clumps of timber, and watered by several small streams. Across a valley I could see a high range thickly wooded, and felt confident that this must be the virgin forest that Dr. Henry's collector had informed me of. By dint of hard work I managed to reach the edge of the forest at 5 P.M., and soon found the house that he told me he had there (altitude 4,700 feet). I have every reason to believe that I was the first European who had ever visited the place, and I may mention that, when I came to stay here later on, natives would make journeys of four or five days to see the Foreign Devil who they heard was living there. Being very tired, I was glad to find a fairly decent house, and after tea turned in early.

On the next day, October 10, I started to reconnoitre and make inquiries of such natives as I might be fortunate enough to meet with, for the district is very thinly populated, the few that do inhabit it growing a little Indian corn for their food, and it is worthy of note that here they will not eat rice. Before I had gone far I came across the tracks of a wild pig, which I followed for some distance, and then, not far from it, found the remains of a domestic pig that had evidently been killed by a leopard, for the tracks could be plainly seen. These I decided to follow, and found they led into the thick jungle, where in most places it was impossible to advance except upon hands and knees. Soon I came upon the lairs of two of them, which they must have very recently quitted, for they were still warm to the hand; probably the brutes had been alarmed at my approach. The jungle now became so thick, and progress so slow, that I was reluctantly obliged to give up the pursuit; and perhaps it would have been wiser never to have attempted it, as they would have been very awkward customers in such a close thicket.

I remained until October 14, by which time I had satisfied myself that the locality was admirably adapted for making collections, provided it was visited at the proper season of the year. I therefore made arrangements to take the house for four months in the following spring and summer, and shall describe the place more fully when dealing with my longer visit. Before leaving I ascended to the ridge of the range, the altitude of which I found to be 6,500 feet, the southern slope being more grassy than the northern. Pheasants were fairly plentiful, both Reeves' and the common, and I shot several before I left.

As it was useless to think of collecting in Chang-yang in the early part of the year, its altitude being too great, I wished to make a short expedition up the river to see what could be done close to its banks. For this purpose the Consul very kindly lent me his house-boat, and in her I left on March 30. I had often heard from the Europeans of an enormous creeping plant not far from the town, but on the opposite side of the river, and I now determined to make a visit to it. When at some little distance off, it presents the appearance of a large mass of dark-green foliage, and on landing I found that there were two separate plants growing just above the high-level water mark of the river, and in such a position that the bases of the trunks would be submerged during floods. These plants formed a truly remarkable sight, the stems being much larger round than a man's body, and growing in a slanting direction; branches are thrown out all round, and creep over a clump of bamboos which support them from the ground, some of the branches reaching to a height of over sixty feet from the surface. They cover a considerable area—not less, in my estimation, than half an acre each. After a diligent search I found a few seeds among the dead leaves on the ground, and one seed pod. As this was not its flowering season, I paid another visit when it was in bloom, and found the blossoms were papilionaceous, about the size round of a florin, and produced in bunches about a foot long from the main stem and principal branches. They were of a deep maroon colour and waxy appearance, the interior being covered with stiff hairs, and are much sought after by hymenopterous insects; so much so, indeed, that their buzzing is almost sufficiently loud to drown ordinary conversation beneath. The seeds are the size of large broad beans, and are contained in pods about six inches long. This remarkable plant is evergreen, and the branches are inhabited by numerous species of birds, amongst which pigeons and several kinds of thrush were most common.

The ground beneath these creepers forms a favourite playground for native children, who carry off the seeds for playthings. Near this a species of soap tree grows, and attains a height of seventy or eighty feet, with a girth of about six feet. Its foliage resembles that of the common ash, but is of a darker green, with the leaves not so pointed. The useful part is the pod, which is gathered, stored, and used, without any further preparation, in the same way and for the same purpose as soap is used. These pods are of a dark-brown colour, and about six inches long. A more highly prized pod is produced on the mountains, and this is shorter but thicker than that grown on the plains. The tree producing it appears to be a species of acacia, judging from the leaf and flower, the latter being yellow. Care must be taken when using this natural soap that the hands are free from cuts or abrasions, for it finds these out at once and causes intense pain. For the same reason it cannot be used for the face, as if a particle enters the eye it is at least half an hour before the pain is got rid of.

Passing up the river, I now entered the Ichang Gorge, where the scenery is magnificent. Instead of low, swampy banks, the river is here confined by mountains and precipices. The towing path is now confined to one side of the river only, and sometimes has to be cut out of the face of a cliff. In the course of a few hours I reached the village of Pin-san-pa, where oranges are cultivated by the natives. This is a small *Le-kin*, or Custom House station, where native boats are examined. After a short stay the journey up the river was resumed, and Shi-pi-san was soon reached. This is a village about fifteen miles from Ichang, situated on the right bank of the river, and at the upper extremity of the gorge.

The river here takes a sharp bend to the northward, and from this point may be seen a range of mountains to the southward and away from the river, which I ascended when on another expedition, but found too much cultivated ground to make it a good collecting station. The first night was passed here, and starting the next morning at 5.30, the bend of the river was followed round, and the same precipitous banks were found, which in some places were very prettily covered with vegetation, among which ferns were conspicuous, till, at 3 P.M., the Mu-tan Rapid was reached, which is remarkable only as being the first on the river. Tracking on till dark, a small village was reached, where the boat was secured for the night.

On proceeding the next morning the Ta-tung Rapid was reached and safely passed, it not being very difficult in the low state of the river, but is dangerous when the water is rising, and also when it is high. The river here widens out considerably, and most of the dangers of the rapids were exposed, many of the huge granite boulders being twenty feet above the water. These are entirely submerged in the spring and summer, and a curious thing to be noticed here, as well as at other rapids on the river, is the way in which deep scores are cut and large holes worn in the hard rocks, the former by the bamboo tracking ropes of generations of boatmen, and the latter made by the constant use of the steel-shod bamboo pole in the same place in fending the boats off. It may be here mentioned that many of the large junks that pass up this rapid have a crew of as many as eighty men.

The scenery is very wild and rocky, and after a hard day's work the boat was made fast for the night at about five miles below the celebrated Sin-tan Rapid. Starting early the next morning the Lu-kan Gorge was passed through, the river now taking a sharp turn to the south, and then, rounding a steep rocky cliff, almost immediately turns to the westward again. This produces a curious effect on ascending the river, as at first glance one is apt to think that further progress is

LU-KAN GORGE.

impossible. The scenery is very fine, as may be seen from the illustration. The gorge is not long, but is dark and gloomy, and soon breaks into a more open country. Here on the left bank a vein of shale about two yards thick crops up, and is worked by the natives. Cormorants may be seen nesting among the crags. Sin-tan was reached at about twelve o'clock, and I saw for the first time this notorious rapid. The boat I was in was too old to venture to make the ascent, and, moreover, was not fitted with the necessary beams. It was low water now, and the most dangerous time at the rapid, for when the river rises sampans and junks may be seen ascending and descending in comparatively smooth water. There is, I believe, sufficient water for a light-draught steamer at all times, but at some little distance out. I gathered from the natives that when the river is at its lowest some of the rocks are visible above the surface.

The most dangerous part is in the centre, where there are many whirlpools, and there is great annual loss of life from drowning. The large junks have at low water to be lightened before passing up, part of the cargo being carried by coolies to the other end of the rapid, where it is re-stowed. Most of the population get their living by tracking and transporting cargoes.

On April 2 I hired a sampan above the rapid and

proceeded up the Me-tan Gorge, where vertical cliffs descend sheer into the water, which is many fathoms deep. It took two hours to reach the other end, where the banks opened and one was able to land. Here I got a few butterflies, but nothing worthy of mention. After tiffin I returned to Sin-tan, and on landing and walking through the village to my boat I twice had sand thrown in my face, and was frequently insulted. I attributed this exhibition of hostility by the natives to their connecting me in some way with a rumour that had reached them of the river being opened to steamer traffic, which, if it ever did happen, would of course seriously damage, if not ruin, their principal source of livelihood. As, however, the Chinese Government have reserved to themselves the right to have the first steamer on this part of the river, it is not likely that it will ever be open to steam navigation. On getting on board there was a fair wind, and a start was made on the return journey. A short distance down a tempting-looking gorge was seen running down to the river, but on landing I found only disappointment awaiting, for I soon found my progress effectually barred by a waterfall tumbling over unclimbable rocks. Close by is one of the extraordinary paths, or rather ladders, made by a series of steps cut into the almost perpendicular surface of the rock, taking advantage of every favourable gradient and ledge, and zig-zagging up in a most curious fashion, sometimes making a very wide sweep to avoid an overhanging spur or perpendicular surface. On attempting it I found that the ascent was very tiring, and the descent extremely difficult, if not dangerous.

On April 3 the homeward journey was continued, and on landing at a gorge I found that I could ascend it and reach some mountains about four miles inland. There was, however, too much cultivated land to make it worth while to collect, indigenous vegetation being found in the glens only. In these are large boulders of grey granite and much iron pyrites. The next day I collected in such glens as I found accessible, and stopped for the night at the village of Nan-too. From this place is seen a range of hills, which are made very conspicuous by having their front of high white cliffs, one being a precipice 2,000 feet deep. The range is crowned with many sharp peaks, one of which is called by the natives the 'Needle of Heaven.'

On April 5 Ichang was again reached, and this short trip concluded.

CHAPTER IV

CHANG-YANG

Preparations for trip to Chang-yang—Hiring coolies—Passport—Start with Dr. Henry—Description of house—Robbery of cash—Collecting Coleoptera—Pony killed by tiger—Tigers common, but no man-eaters—Poisoning tigers—Wild pigs—Boars' tusks offered for sale as tigers' teeth—Deer—Porcupines—Pheasants—Plants and flowers—Hostility of natives—I complain at Ichang—Punishment of agitators—Excursion to the South—Deep ravines—Etu River—Varnish tree—Method of collecting varnish—Trade of district—Edible fungus—Heavy damages—Preparation for return to Ichang.

As the time now approached for my projected stay in Chang-yang, I commenced making such preparations as were necessary for a prolonged visit to such a wild region. The first thing to be considered was money. Silver would, of course, be much easier to carry than thousands of cash, but I had learnt from my previous visit that it was far too valuable for use among such a poor people. If change of a tael was wanted, one might have to send to a village half a day's journey off to get it. The natives also were particular as to the sort of cash they would accept, being partial to the large, not that they would not take the small, but they regarded them as of comparatively less value. I therefore made arrangements to get as many thousands of the large cash as I thought I should require from the bankers and merchants. Their weight was considerable, and the cost of transport added not a little to the expense of the journey up.

I then saw to my collecting boxes, cases, &c., all of which were made of teak, the only wood I found serviceable in the damp climate in which I was to live for four months. For firearms I had a double 12, a small collecting gun, a Winchester repeater, and a revolver. I also laid in a stock of tinned provisions, as from former experience I found that nothing eatable, except Indian corn and millet, was to be had I was afterwards much disappointed with these, as a large proportion turned out to be bad.

These things, together with my clothing, bedding, nets, &c., made loads for fifteen coolies. It is never advisable to hire these in the street, but to go to a *hong*, where no doubt a little more has to be paid, but then a written agreement can be made with the manager, whereby he is made responsible for the honesty of the men he may send you, and be held liable in case of theft. It should also be stipulated that a head coolie is sent for every seven to ten men, who is, again, made responsible for the men under his charge. He is paid at the same rate as the others, but carries a lighter load, and his duties are to keep his men up to their work, and make all arrangements for their feeding, &c. It is always usual to give a *cumshaw* or present at the end of a journey if the men have behaved themselves well. The hongs where coolies are to be engaged are licensed by the local government.

My passport for the province of Hu-peh having been already obtained at Hankow, and all being ready for a start, I left Ichang on April 16, accompanied by Dr. Henry as far as the barrier, he having obtained three months' leave, which he intended to spend in a botanical and exploring trip all round Ichang.

The journey to Chang-yang has been described before, and the only difference between this and the former journey was, that it occupied four days instead of three, I arriving at my destination on April 20.

Here I found that the house had been cleared out and cleaned for my reception. It was about 30 feet by 20 feet, with mud walls about 12 feet high, and had an earthen floor and a thatched roof, but no internal divisions. This was inconvenient, and as soon as possible I got a rough native carpenter in, and made him build a partition right across from the ridge to the floor. In the partition I had a door fitted with a lock, so that my collections, money, and other valuables might be kept in reasonable security; and as this private room of mine was fairly lofty, I had a boarded floor put in, about eight feet from the ground, and ascended to it by means of a ladder from the outside. This I made my bedroom, and when the arrangements were completed, found myself fairly comfortable. In the outer room the cooking was done, and here the coolies, collectors, &c., assembled. The outer doors were secured on the inside by two stout pieces of timber sliding across as a protection against robbers, who are reputed to be common in this particularly wild region.

The day after my arrival I paid off and discharged the Ichang coolies, keeping only my cook and interpreter and a boy with me. Soon after their departure I found that the large cash I had been to such trouble to secure had all been changed for small, and upon inquiry discovered that the thief was a native of the district, who had come down by arrangement to assist and act as a guide to my coolies. I blamed myself very much for having trusted him with such a valuable load, which, if it had been taken by a coolie engaged from the hong, would in all probability have been delivered untampered with. The thief naturally kept out of my way, and I was unable to afford time to trace him out and have punishment administered, which was unfortunate, as it set a bad example to the other natives, who might think they could treat me in the same way.

It was now wet weather, and too early for butterflies; but my time was fully occupied in getting the native collectors acquainted with the work I wished of them, establishing different stations, &c., and then in spare time beating the flowering bushes, with a light but closely woven circular basket held underneath, to collect the small, but highly interesting, coleopterous insects that abound in such places. I felt convinced that the place would eventually prove rich in Lepidoptera, and in this I was not disappointed.

On April 23 I was informed that a tiger had killed a pony, and upon proceeding to the spot found the pony to be one that my boy and myself had noticed feeding the day before. The tiger must have been an enormous brute, as his footmarks measured 5½ inches across. I found during my stay that tigers are very numerous in this district, and that they do much damage to the live-stock of the natives, which consists of horses, ponies, cows, and pigs. They never, as far as I could learn, attack human beings, and the natives are strangely careless in the protection of their live-stock. Pigs, for example, are usually kept in a small bamboo pen by the side of the hut, and if one is taken out by a tiger, the owner will replace it as soon as he is able; but the idea of using a few more bamboos in making the pen or sty secure against another attack, does not appear to enter into his head. Poison is used to destroy them, as well as leopards, in the following manner. When the remains of an animal that has been killed are found, an incision is made down the back of the neck, and the skin drawn aside. Two powders are then rubbed in, the first, of which a considerable quantity is used, being of an emerald-green colour; the other is white, and not much (perhaps an ounce) is considered sufficient. I was unable to find out what these powders consisted of, and it would be interesting to know, for they are undoubtedly very effective in poisoning the tigers or leopards, whose flesh is invariably devoured again by their poisoners, after having been boiled in two or three waters, and, as far as I could hear, without any ill-effects following.

On visiting a carcass that has been poisoned, the natives arm themselves with long spears, the only occasion on which they are carried except when in the pursuit of wild pig. Many people in China assured me that pigs and tigers are never found together in the same locality, but I am convinced they are mistaken, as here they both occurred plentifully, and leopards as well. In small covers and jungles it is quite possible that the presence of a tiger or leopard might cause a general exodus of the pigs; but in forest lands, such as are found here, they exist together in numbers. The only tiger that I saw here destroyed by poison had killed a pig on June 28, and partly eaten it. The remains were poisoned in the manner previously described, and left till the next morning, when, on approaching, the brute was seen about a hundred yards from its prey in a helpless, cramped condition, and it very soon died. It proved to be a fine young male, and measured as follows: Tip of nose to base of tail, 66 inches; tail, 34 inches; round head, 29 inches; round neck, 23 inches; round fore-arm, 28 inches; length of fore-leg, 26 inches; round fore-foot, 13½ inches; length of hind leg, 29½ inches; round hind foot, 10 inches. Eight coolies were required to carry the carcass to the house, where it was triced up to a beam and skinned. This operation, together with cutting the flesh off the bones, took a great part of the night; the latter was undertaken as I wished to preserve the skeleton.

The meat, &c., was all carried off and devoured, the bones being put to macerate; and now a new difficulty presented itself to me. This was how to prevent their being stolen, as they are worth at least thirty taels, and are used partly in medicine. Some are supposed to be most effective in strengthening the muscles on which they are rubbed, a rounded bone of the hind leg being much prized for this purpose. I therefore kept them in a tub of water in the house until my nostrils rebelled.

They were then put out of doors at some distance away; but I was obliged to have a coolie on guard day and night over the tub, and owing to these precautions I managed to keep the skeleton entire.

To show how common tigers are, I may mention that this tiger was killed on June 29, and on July 2 a tiger killed a pony, both of these being close to my house, while from a hamlet about two miles distant, and situated over a spur of the mountain, I had almost daily reports of domestic animals, such as ponies, oxen, and pigs, being killed by tigers or leopards.

Wild pigs are common, and do much damage at night in the fields of Indian corn, the mischief most frequently being done when the grain is ripe or nearly so. At this time they are sometimes surprised by the natives and killed with the long spears mentioned before. At other times they are marked into detached patches of jungle or small woods, and surrounded and killed.

One day a native brought me two wild boars' tusks and some of the fine, almost bristle-like, quills of the porcupine. These he wished to sell to me, saying they were the teeth and whiskers of an enormous tiger. He asked a fabulous price for them; but upon my telling him to what animals they had once belonged, he eventually offered to make me a present of them.

A small species of deer is found in the rocky parts of the forest, which are very difficult of access. They are far from being common, but on one occasion a specimen was brought in alive, which I purchased. Unfortunately, I failed to keep it for long.

Porcupines are common, living among the rocks, but being nocturnal in their habits are not often seen. Their quills may be frequently picked up, and numbers were brought in by my collectors. I also obtained a young specimen alive, and sent it to Mr. Montgomery at Ichang, where it lived and thrived.

Golden pheasants were not found near my house, but at a place about two days' journey distant appeared to be numerous, as many were brought to me alive, having been snared by the leg. The common and Reeves' pheasants were plentiful where I lived, and I occasionally shot them to vary my diet of Indian corn-cake, but being out of season they were not very palatable. These also were caught by the natives in snares. I noticed a species of woodcock here, but it was not by any means common.

The poppy is cultivated in the valleys for the production of opium, which is used principally to barter for goods brought from the towns.

In May and June the cuckoo may be heard, reminding one of home, and the air is loaded with the fragrance of the honeysuckle. Azaleas grow to a height of from twelve to fourteen feet, and are covered with pink blossoms. There is also a very fine clematis running over the rocks. Higher up in the forest, rhododendrons are found growing luxuriantly and in many fine varieties, some specimens being twenty feet high and bearing large white fragrant blossoms. Towards the north the country is much broken; range after range could be seen on a clear day from my mud house. Looking to the west, the spurs are covered with dense forest, and I remember on one particular moonlight night the black forest standing out against the horizon, the loneliness, isolation and wildness of the scene were most impressive.

After residing for two months here, reports were constantly reaching me that the natives had convinced themselves that my stay would bring them bad luck. One day I found a disorderly crowd at my house, and heard that a big meeting was to be held the following day to consider what steps should be taken to remove me. Two days later I found notices pasted on the trees all round, to the effect that any native who was found to be collecting for me, or assisting me in any way, would be bambooed, and stating that I was bringing bad luck to the district. At the same time I was threatened that, if I did not remove immediately,

I should be tied up to a tree and beaten. Under these circumstances my work came to a standstill, but I felt sure that the state of affairs could be remedied by application to the proper authority. Leaving all my things in the house in charge of the interpreter, I started for Ichang, with one coolie only, on July 28, and travelling light, made the journey in two days. Here I at once went to her Majesty's Consul (Mr. Gregory), who at my request reported the state of affairs to the prefect of the town. Letters were immediately sent by him to the magistrate at Chang-yang by special runners; and after making sure that these were well on their way, I started on my return journey on August 5, as I was especially anxious not to lose any time. I was again only two days on the road, and on arriving found the house safe and everything quiet; the object of my journey being known, had somewhat damped the ardour of some of the more prominent agitators. On August 12 seven men arrived bearing a despatch for me from the Chang-yang magistrate. They asked me to explain everything to them, and after having done so and also indicated the ringleaders of the disturbance, they squeezed them to the extent of several thousand cash (a considerable sum for such poor people), and had notices put up throughout the district, in every village and hamlet, commanding that I was to be left at peace.

Having done this they left, and I had no more trouble of the sort, everything going on smoothly and all the collectors rejoining my service. The weather was, however, now beginning to get cold, with heavy rain, showing plainly that the season for collecting was drawing to a close, and that I should soon have to return. I decided before going to make an excursion over the summit of the range and into the valley beyond. When I got to the ridge I saw that the country to the southward was much more open, there being no forest; the surface also was more cultivated, and there were no more mountain ranges near, but it was much cut up by deep ravines and watercourses, which were rich in beautiful plants, flowers, and ferns. It is no exaggeration to say that it is quite possible to talk to a man across one of these ravines when it would perhaps take two days' journey to reach him, so deep and precipitous are they and dangerous to traverse. The watercourses, which are very numerous, form tributaries of the Etu River, which enters the Yang-tze twenty miles below Ichang, and is navigable for sampans only for some distance from its mouth. Here is found the tree whose sap produces vegetable varnish (*Rhus vernicifera?*). It grows to about the size of an ordinary ash or walnut on the sides of the slopes at considerable elevation. In the month of May longitudinal incisions are made in the trunk and limbs, and at the lower end of each is inserted the shell of a species of freshwater mussel, into which the sap, which is of the consistence of thick cream, flows. These are carefully emptied into a wooden bucket every morning, and the bleeding is continued for about a fortnight. The quantity of sap produced from each incision is very small, and it takes a long time to half fill the bucket. The collectors suffer from a severe form of rash. This varnish is an article of considerable importance, and forms with walnuts, which are produced in quantities, and a small quantity of opium, the only articles of commerce. Tea of a very inferior quality, the commonest pottery, and coarse native cotton cloth are the only articles brought into this poor and primitive region, where the system of barter generally prevails. In this neighbourhood a certain species of glutinous-looking fungus is found growing in lumps on various sorts of trees in damp places, and this is much appreciated as an article of food. My coolies collected as much as they could, and after consuming what they wished, took the remainder to Ichang to give to their friends or to sell. My expedition to the south extended over three days, and on my return to the house I commenced to make preparations for a return to Ichang. I could congratulate myself upon having made a very satisfactory collection in spite of the difficulties that were put in my way. Those that have been mentioned were not the only ones, and as a further illustration of the way in which I was treated, on one occasion one of my men, collecting a large species of Ornithoptera, unfortunately damaged a few shoots of growing Indian corn, doing harm to the extent probably of twenty cash. An old woman came up, and poured forth upon us some of the most flowery portions of the Chinese language with such volubility and persistence that she caused a crowd to collect, and to avoid a disturbance I was obliged to pay 2,000 cash. It took some time getting everything together and packed, getting the apparatus from the native collectors, and especially seeing to the bottles containing cyanide (as to leave these among such a careless and ignorant people would be culpable), and arranging for stationing collectors for the following season. At last, having completed everything, I left for Ichang, and took four days over the journey. I found the river very high, and the current so strong that the boat was swept down two miles and had to be tracked up on the other side.

CHAPTER V

SHA-SHIH AND PA-CHOW

Excursion to Sha-shih—Large town with considerable trade—Ravages of cholera—Ho-sia—Try to find lakes, but fail—Trouble at a village—False information—Further insults—Treachery of coolies—Arrival at boat—Sturgeon—Stopped by head wind—Washing for gold—Tiger's Tooth Gorge—Loss of silver-laden junk—Return to Shanghai with Mrs. Pratt—Purchase cases for collections and duck-guns—Wild-fowl on Yang-tze—Return to Ichang—Floods—Decrease in size of river above Tung-ting Lakes—Arrive at Ichang—Contract for boat to be built—Delay in building—Trip to Pa-chow—Cranes and storks at Hope Island—Geese at Pa-chow—Etu—Return to Ichang—Departure of Mrs. Pratt and children for England—Description of boat and arrangements on board.

My collections from Chang-yang were now finally looked over, packed up, and despatched home. When this was finished several excursions were made down the river, and such as might interest the reader will be described.

On November 17, the Consul having kindly offered me the use of his house-boat, I went down to Sha-shih, which is eighty miles from Ichang, and being with the current, the journey was made in one day. I stayed at this place for a few hours, and found two English missionaries, Mr. and Mrs. Gulston; the former kindly accompanied me through the town. It is a place of considerable size, having a population of about 100,000, and has fine streets and shops for a Chinese town. It is a large trade centre, and at certain seasons hundreds of junks may be seen waiting for the water to fall, in order to proceed up the river. They form rows nearly two miles long, and thickly packed off the town; their cargoes being principally cotton goods for the up-river ports. Mr. Gulston informed me that last year the cholera worked terrific destruction among the inhabitants of the town, and that the stench from the corpses was almost unbearable, the Chinese custom being to allow a considerable time to elapse between death and interment, without taking into any consideration the state of the weather.

Continuing down the stream, I arrived at Ho-sia, thirty miles further, on the 19th. Having heard that there were some lakes inland that were much frequented by wading birds, I wished to visit them and have some shooting, if possible. I landed with one of my men and, with the intention of spending the night on shore, hired a coolie, who professed to know the way, to carry my things. After several hours' walk through a very fertile country in which tobacco and sugar are largely grown, and seeing no traces of the lakes, he brought me to a large and thickly populated village, where I found the inhabitants very badly disposed towards foreigners.

Here I was stoned and insulted, but getting away as quickly as possible, proceeded with the coolie in further search of the lakes. He proved to be an utter impostor, for I never saw a lake the whole day, and after another walk of some distance found myself in a small village, where I was told by the peasants that by means of a stream near I could get down to the river in a sampan to within a short distance of the place where the house-boat lay. I have no hesitation in saying that I was deliberately deceived by false information, for on proceeding in the direction indicated, no stream could be found. I now found a fresh difficulty, for the coolie threw down my things and refused to carry them any further.

A crowd quickly assembled, and I found myself in a most disagreeable position, for they were anything but friendly, and again stones and mud were thrown at me. The man I had brought from the boat ultimately found two men to do the work of the one who had struck, and I engaged them at an exorbitant wage, for I was quite at their mercy. Before they had gone far they put down their loads and refused to proceed further unless paid 400 cash, and to this demand I felt obliged to yield. A little further on they just put the loads down and left me. For the third time I was in a crowd of natives, who appear to quickly assemble in cases of the sort, and after more mud-throwing and insults, my boatman got two coolies who eventually carried my things down to the boat, where I arrived at 11.30 P.M., after a most disagreeable time, and having had nothing to eat all day. The farmhouses in the district through which I passed appeared to be better and more substantially built than usual; but the natives are undoubtedly hostile to Europeans, and, among other things, they are given to assemble on the banks of the river to pelt with stones the steamers running between Hankow and Ichang.

On November 20 I commenced my return journey up the stream, and after a few miles found a fisherman with a freshly-caught sturgeon still alive. This is the fish which, as I have mentioned before, I was unable to purchase. It weighed about 200 catties (260 lbs.), and was between eight and nine feet long. The captor had hauled it up on the bank previous to cutting it up for sale. The boat was secured for the night at a village called Da-ku, and on trying to proceed the next morning I found that the wind was too strong to allow tracking up-stream, so the boat was huloed over to the other side to try on the more sheltered bank; but it was of no use, and she had to be secured in a creek until the gale subsided. While here, I witnessed for the first time the interesting operation of washing for gold, which is carried on more or less all up the river. About forty men were engaged at this part, and worked in pairs, one man being employed in digging the earth out of the bank and carrying it to the other, who worked the washing apparatus, which was of very crude construction. It consisted of a basket slung so as to be easily rocked, and of coarse construction, having a wooden lever attached to rock it with. Underneath was a board about six feet long by four broad, in which were cut a number of transverse grooves. This was fixed in an inclined position, the upper part being under the rocking-basket. The earth was tipped into the basket, the man attending working the lever with one hand, while with the other he threw water into it. The contents being thus washed through, ran down the inclined board, the black sand and gold dust lodging in the grooves, and the lighter soil being washed away. About every four hours the grooves were scraped out, and the dust and sand collected in small bags for transport home, when it would be treated with mercury to collect the gold. The amount recovered, however, is very small, and I understood that the average daily earnings were about 100 cash per man—say 3½*d.* in English money. Only a Chinese could live upon such a sum, and yet there are thousands so engaged in the upper parts of the river.

The next day, the wind having moderated, I was able to continue my return voyage up the river, and arrived at Sha-shih at about 3 P.M. Proceeding upwards again the next day, I stopped at what is called the Tiger's Tooth Gorge. This is not a gorge in the proper sense of the word at all, but simply some hills which come close to the river banks. On the right bank there is a curious natural bridge at a considerable elevation, so high that from the river the sky may be seen underneath it. Some years ago a junk laden with a large quantity of shoe silver, the property of the Government, was wrecked near here; but although many attempts were made to recover her valuable cargo they all proved fruitless, not a single piece of silver being ever recovered.

I found on my return that my wife was suffering from a severe attack of fever. She was, indeed, so seriously ill that I considered it necessary to take her to Shanghai for medical advice, and we therefore embarked in the next steamer for Hankow. Provided that the shoals near Sunday Island are passed without the boat getting aground, the passage usually takes about three days, but if the steamer should happen to get ashore, she may stop there for some days. At

Hankow a change is made into a larger steamer, and after three days more Shanghai is reached.

Here I at once set about getting a supply of tin-lined cases for the collection I proposed to make in the far west of China and in Tibet. These are made very well in Shanghai, but I was unable to get them at Ichang. I was also fortunate enough to be able to buy two large-bore shoulder duck-guns, such things not usually being found for sale here. The Yang-tze-kiang is the home of myriads of wild-fowl of many kinds, and in the lower part of the river, especially at a place called Wu-hu, they are shot with comparative ease, as there are, as a rule, plenty of reeds, rushes, &c., which afford some cover. Further up the river, however, things change considerably, for there are generally plenty of wild-fowl and little or no cover. They are, therefore, very difficult to approach, and an ordinary 12-bore is not of much use. I took one of these duck-guns afterwards into Tibet, where it proved to be of the greatest possible service.

After a stay of a month at Shanghai my wife had nearly recovered from her attack of fever, and I now thought it would be safe to return up the river and prepare for my most important trip—that to Tibet, if I could get as far. The journey up is a more tedious affair than the journey down, and takes from ten days to three weeks to accomplish, the time being according to the strength of current which has to be combated. When the river is high the current is strong, and may be augmented by flood water from certain districts, and the floods, unless caused by the melting of the snow in the upper part of the river, are nearly always local, the breadth of the river bed gradually reducing the apparent volume of water as it passes down towards the sea. Thus Ichang may be in flood, and at Hankow only a slight rise may be observed; and Hankow may be flooded from the Han River and Tung-ting Lakes, while a slight rise only is noted in the lower reaches, where the river widens considerably. Another cause of delay in the upward journey is the uncertainty of finding the steamer for the upper river ready at Hankow. Passengers may have to wait there for three or four days.

After leaving Hankow we soon came to the mouth of the Tung-ting Lakes, and saw many of the boats for which the district is well known. These are very clean, small, and narrow, and are half-decked, by which peculiarities they may be easily recognised among the other river-trading boats. It is worthy of note that the river traffic seems to increase quite 100 per cent. below the entrance to these lakes, indicating that there is a large inland trade through them. The river decreases in volume very much after passing the entrance, and though I made every endeavour to find out something about the district in which they are situated, I failed to get any reliable information. That an enormous trade takes place through them is evident; but as far as I could find out, they had not been explored to their southern limits by any European for many years, if ever, and the rivers running into them run from the province of Quei-chow, nearly touching the borders of Quang-si and Quang-tung. This is irrespective of the province of Hoo-nan, in which the lakes are situated, so it is evident that they form a road to the Yang-tze-kiang from at least four large provinces.

On my arrival at Ichang, I commenced by trying to find a boat suitable for my purpose to ascend to Kia-ting-fu, and having sufficient room for the storage of collections, &c. It was soon evident that nothing was to be bought that was in any way desirable, and I had no intention of hiring, as I wished on arrival at the town mentioned to discharge the greater part of the crew, and keep the boat afloat as a sort of base to which I could send my things as fast as they were collected. Nothing remained, then, but to have such a boat as I required built, and as soon as possible I had rough specifications drawn up, and asked contractors to give a price. After a fortnight this was to all appearance settled satisfactorily, I having given the contract to a native builder, and with the promise of a premium for each day she was in the water before a certain date, he at the same time being liable to a corresponding fine for each day she was late.

The work was now commenced, but before any progress had been made to speak of, a rival builder, whose claim was that he had always before constructed boats for the Europeans, appeared upon the scene, and tried to assert his claims to have the work put into his hands. Finding that his demands received no attention, he collected a band of such riffraff as he could find, and did all he could to hinder my man at his work, and it was only after an appeal to the Consul that this obstruction was put a stop to by his representation to the prefect of the town. This disturbance, I may mention, caused a cessation of work for a fortnight. I should here say that my contract was for a boat about 36 feet on the water-line, to be built of pine, with 10 feet beam, and having a flat floor and long counter, the only difference in the construction of the actual hull from that of the ordinary native gunboats being that on each side of the timbers, which were of a red wood resembling juniper, there should be a good knee of the same wood, the ordinary practice being to have one only. I stipulated for this extra strengthening because, as it may be remembered, I had gone up to the Sin-tan Rapids before, and was able to see the amount of knocking about a boat might have to go through. She was only to draw about two feet of water when fully loaded, and to be fitted for ascending all the rapids that might be met with.

Having seen the boat fairly started in building, I was able to take a trip down the river to an island called Pa-chow, about thirty miles from Ichang. I went with Mr. Montgomery in his boat, and having the duck-guns with us as well as the smaller bores, we got at Swain's Shoal, within sight of the town, a shot with one of the former, which resulted in bagging five teal and two ducks. Proceeding further down we got to Hope Island, which is from four to five miles long, with ponds in the centre, but having no cover to speak of. It is frequented by wild-fowl of many species, but more especially by a very large species of crane, one of which I was anxious to secure as a specimen. In this I was disappointed, for it seemed impossible to get within range on such flat ground. This crane, and also a stork marked in a very striking manner with black and white, were frequently seen on various parts of the river in this district, but, often as I tried, I was unable to obtain a specimen of either. On the island were to be seen many cranes, storks, pelicans, and eagles.

After getting a few ducks only, we went on to Pa-chow. This island is in great part submerged when the river is high, and is situated near the right bank of the Yang-tze-kiang. There is a passage for native craft between it and the shore at all times, but as the river subsides the sands are very dangerous, being quick, or running, until the water has drained out of them. They are then hard, and quite safe.

The island may be from seven to ten miles long, and is sparingly inhabited, there being a few hamlets only. The natives occupy themselves as agriculturists or fishermen, but are all very poor. Numbers of grey geese are seen on the banks, but they are very difficult to approach. At mid-day they may be seen in large flocks resting on the dry sands in the higher parts of the island. At night they go inland to the corn-fields to feed, and do much damage to the crops. Cranes and storks of the same species that were seen at Hope Island were also seen here plentifully, and a small species of turkey buzzard also. Deer occur sparingly on the island, and are not easily shot. They are of a small species. On the bank of the river opposite the island very good pheasant shooting used to be had, but it has now been ruined by the Chinese, who have destroyed the cover.

We now commenced our return, and on the way up

the river stopped at Etu, twenty miles below Ichang, which is situated on the bank of a river flowing into the Yang-tze, and which I had on a former occasion ascended for about ten miles in a steam launch. The town stands high up on the right bank, well out of the way of floods, and a considerable trade is carried on with Ichang in the vegetable varnish before mentioned, opium, and garden produce. The banks of the river Etu are rocky and rugged, but every available spot is cultivated. The water (except during floods) is remarkably clear, and the bottom of stones and shingle. On the left bank of the Yang-tze, and nearly opposite to the town of Etu, a branch from the main road from Pekin comes down to the river bank.

On my return to Ichang I found the boat progressing satisfactorily; but before giving a description of how she was fitted up, I should say that, having heard of the most unsettled state of the country about Chung-king and its humid and unhealthy climate, I decided not to take my wife and little ones up there as I had originally intended, but to send them all home. I therefore arranged for their passage, saw all the packing done, and regretfully saw them off for home on March 22.

The boat upon which I was to depend so much had now better be more fully described. To commence with the most important part after the hull, which was, in my opinion, the cabin. This was about sixteen feet long by eight broad, with nearly seven feet head room. Owing to the flat nature of the floor of the boat there were no awkward triangular lockers or cupboards, but the whole inside was as square as a room in a house ashore, and was thus available to be made use of in the most advantageous manner for shelves and lockers. A doorway was fitted at the fore and after ends, with a booby-hatch over each and steps leading down from the deck (for the floor of the cabin was only four inches from the flat bottom of the boat), a ventilator being fitted above. The roof was slightly rounded and covered with English sail-cloth well painted; windows were fitted at the sides, to which were attached wooden blinds. There was a gangway space of a foot on each side of the cabin, forming a deck plank or waterway to the gunwale. Just before and just abaft the cabin were secured by lashings to the frame of the boat two athwartships spars of about six inches in diameter, and projecting a foot beyond either gunwale. Great care was taken in their fitting and securing, as they play an important part in the tracking up-stream as well as being a support for the huloes or sculls, which are worked on a small pin driven into their outer ends. The huloes were about thirty feet long and made in two pieces, the blade and the loom. The blade is a plank or board about nine inches wide, and bound with iron at the outer end to prevent splitting. The inner end is narrower, and is joined to the loom by iron bolts and hoops. A collar which has a loose hole for the pin to work in is lashed on. As there were two spars there was room for four huloes; but, unfortunately, on starting I was only provided with two, and later on one of these breaking when in a dangerous place, put the boat in a perilous position. All boats should be provided with at least two spare huloes.

Just before the cabin the mast was stepped, and on this there was fitted to set, when the wind was favourable, a Chinese lug sail made of native cotton canvas. All the fore part was decked in flush with the gunwale and had two hatchways fitted. This fore hold was nearly four feet deep, and was most useful for stowing cables and stores in. In wet or cold weather also the crew used to go down and sleep there, but in fine weather they had a light bamboo frame to cover over the fore part of the boat, and mats being thrown over this, it formed quite sufficient shelter. Across the bows of the boat there was built a strong beam of hard wood hooped with iron, and fitted with two thole-pins in the centre for the bow sweep.

The Chinese builders in choosing a piece of wood for this beam always give the preference to one that

BOAT READY FOR THE VOYAGE.

has a crooked grain, saying that it is stronger. The bow sweep that works on this beam is a spar suitable to the size of the boat, with the thick end inboard, and on to the thin end are secured by lashings, or bolts, or both, two narrow but thick blades. The spar is fitted at the inboard end with beckets and heel ropes according to its size. Mine was only about thirty feet long; but many of the large junks have them of nearly sixty feet in length, and manned by about forty men or more. They are absolutely indispensable in the navigation of the rapids, and are, as far as I am aware, only in use in China. By their skilful use boats may be turned quickly in the strongest current, and although clumsy-looking, are perhaps the most useful things in the boat when coming down-stream in a flood.

Abaft the cabin the boat was again decked to the counter, and under the deck were two lockers, one for a store and the other for the cooking utensils of the crew, which were very simple. The tiller nearly touched the cabin door, and my skipper, though a very worthy and good man, was so short that I was obliged to have a special stool made for him to stand on, to enable him to see over the roof of the cabin. On the high counter was built the cook-house, where my provisions were cooked, and in which the cook and my boy slept. The whole of the boat was varnished with the vegetable varnish before mentioned, which is universally used for this purpose in China. I had, however, the cabin and topsides painted white in addition, as I thought it would be cooler. This answered very well from my point of view, but was a failure in another, as will be seen later on.

CHAPTER VI

THROUGH THE GORGES OF THE YANG-TZE

Captain and crew of boat—Trackers—Stores taken—Start up the river—Ta-tung Rapid—Life-boats—Wreck passed—Sin-tan Rapid—An anxious night—Me-tan Gorge—Kwei—Yeh-tan Rapid—Pa-tung-hsien—Wild rose—Absence of birds—Wu-shan Gorge—Fung-sien Gorge—Accident in a rapid—Striking scenery—Chinese coffins—Road making—Brine springs—Quei-chow-fu—Examination of passports—Trade of the place—Escort—Dog overboard—Bad rapid—Riverside villages—Wan-hsien—Opportunity to send letters—Orange trees—St. George's Island—Lung-chau.

THE boat being now ready, my next consideration was to get a captain and crew. The former I succeeded in getting through the Commissioner of Customs, and he stayed with me for two years, proving himself to be a good man and very capable of taking charge of the boat in the most dangerous places. To him I left principally the selection of the crew, which consisted of eight boatmen and eight trackers. The last have severely hard work going up-river, and dangerous work too. Paths, perhaps a hundred feet above the water and barely eighteen inches wide, are often all he has to work upon, and in such places, if the boat should make a sudden outward sheer and he cannot quickly disengage himself from the tracking rope by slipping the toggle, which connects it to the tracking band on the shoulder, he is very likely to be dragged over the cliff. A sullen plunge, and in the river by which he has made his livelihood he finds his grave. Bodies are frequently seen floating about, but they are carefully avoided by the natives. This crew, with an assistant collector sent out from home, a German named Krichel-dorff, and my cook-interpreter and boy, made with myself twenty-one hands on board—close packing for such a small craft—but before going very far I was obliged to increase the number.

I now had the lockers and shelves in the cabin well stocked with boxes of a suitable size for holding such specimens as I hoped to obtain, and these, with about seventy butterfly nets for distribution among the local collectors I intended to engage, chemicals, medicine, botanical drying paper, papers for Lepidoptera, and tins for Coleoptera, took up a good deal of room, and the remainder was taken up by tinned provisions, photographic apparatus, clothing, and my guns and ammunition. The firearms consisted of a 12- and a 4-bore shot guns, a small collecting gun, and a Winchester repeating rifle. Bamboo tracking ropes of great length and several sizes were coiled away in the hold or on the counter out of the way. These are of great strength, provided that no kinks are taken in them, but with a short nip they snap at once. They are in universal use on the river for tracking, and, owing to the sharp edges of the bamboo, are somewhat dangerous to use unless handled with great care. I had also on board an anchor and a $\frac{3}{8}$-inch chain cable, which I had purchased at Shanghai for use in case of emergency.

After having seen all ready, a start was made at 4.30 P.M. on March 26, with a fair wind upstream. Everything, however, was not in its place, for one of the crew was ashore. He came off hurriedly, seeing the boat under way, and in getting out of the sampan fell overboard, but was promptly picked up, with no damage done beyond getting wet through. The steamer *Kiang-tung* was at anchor in the river, and as we passed her the captain saluted with a blast of the steam whistle, the last sound of the sort we heard for many months. After getting well away from the town, I had the boat anchored for the night opposite the mouth of the Unknown River. This is a small stream, and takes its name from the fact that none of the European inhabitants of Ichang have as yet ascended it. The Chinese always make a point of taking a short distance as the day's journey on making a start for a long trip, and I was quite prepared for an early halt, only taking care that I was far enough from the town to prevent any of the crew or trackers returning there that night.

The next morning a start was made at 4.45 A.M., and the trackers had to work for several hours. At last a fair breeze sprung up, and we were able to proceed under sail until arriving at a small village ninety li from Ichang, where the boat was made fast for the night. This place was reached at 5.30 P.M., and I had been busy all day rearranging the various things in the cabin and seeing that those articles which might be wanted in a hurry were stowed in accessible places. On March 28 we were under way at 4.54 A.M. with a fair wind, which, however, soon died away, and the trackers had to be landed to tow against the stream. We were now approaching the Ta-tung Rapid, where the rocks and boulders are extremely dangerous. Here was one of the life-boats whose duty it is to pick up all bodies floating in the river, and to save life if possible. They get paid, I believe, so much for each one brought on shore, whether living or dead. They are usually manned by five men, and are easily known as they are always painted red. The Government supplies them and their crew, and they are stationed in the dangerous parts of the river. The current was found to be very strong, and this, combined with a head wind, compelled us to anchor for some hours. Later on we managed to make a short advance, but were obliged eventually to make fast to the bank just below the rapid.

Making a start at 4.45 the next morning, it took nearly three hours to get against the strong current to the foot of the rapid. Here more trackers had to be engaged, and it took fifteen to get the boat through. I hoped to reach the Sin-tan Rapid during the day, as there were no bad places to pass. The wreck of a large house-boat was seen in the forenoon, she having come to grief about three days previously.

Such wrecks are very common, and it is impossible to make any estimate of the number of men drowned in the river, but it must be very large. The thermometer to-day registered 85°. The Sin-tan Rapid was reached at 1.30 P.M., and I found that the boat would have to be unloaded before the ascent was attempted, not on account of the shallowness of the river, but to make her tow more easily against the current, which was very violent, but with no actual fall that I could see. This afternoon a junk was wrecked, but happily no lives were lost. A sandstorm raged all day, and everything in the boat was covered with very fine sand which seemed to penetrate everywhere. Just before arriving here one of my men cut his thumb severely through carelessly handling a bamboo hawser. The muscles were cut round down to the bone. I dressed it as well as I could with lint and carbolic lotion, and kept him on board in the hope it might heal. This, however, it did not do so rapidly as I expected, and I had, in the end, to land him and get another man in his place.

On March 30 commenced unloading the boat at 6 A.M., sending everything by coolies to a shed built for the purpose at the head of the rapid. The boat then had to await her turn to be towed up, and this caused a delay of eleven hours. There were thirty men on the tow rope, and even then the progress was made by inches. Though the rapid was only about 220 yards long the ascent took till 5.30 P.M., so some idea may be formed of the violence of the current. As soon as the top was reached the reloading commenced, and this took till dark. My boat was the first owned by a European that had made the ascent, and knowing from former experience the feeling of the natives towards foreigners, I took especial care in seeing her secured for the night. Two anchors were laid out, to one of which was secured the chain cable (a thing hardly ever seen in native boats), and a watch was kept all night to guard against treachery, for they would have had no hesitation in cutting us adrift, if possible, and sending us down the rapid to destruction. The sandstorm continued all day, and the river was at its lowest.

THE SIN-TAN RAPID. RIVER LOW.

On the 31st, after a most uneasy night, a start was made at 7.30 A.M. It was a rainy morning, and the trackers had hard work to get through the Me-tan Gorge. The cliffs here are 150 feet high. Stopped at Kwei, and here, to avoid hiring extra men so often to help through the rapids, I engaged three more permanently. There are many bad places about here, and at certain seasons, when the river is high, a very dangerous rapid, in which many lives are lost. Last year the mail boat was wrecked, all the mails lost, and two men drowned. There was no wind all day, and the trackers had hard work.

April 1.—Started at 6 A.M. and found the current very strong. At 9 A.M., after three hours' work, I found that we had only made fifteen li. The Yeh-tan Rapid was reached at three in the afternoon. It was not very bad in the present state of the river, but is reported to be dangerous at certain times. The current is always strong. Half an hour afterwards another short rapid was reached, and here the river was certainly narrower than I had ever before seen it. Though the wind was favourable, it took thirty men to tow the boat up against the strong current. Pa-tung-hsien was reached at 7.30 P.M. It is situated on the right bank of the river, and was, by my captain's statement, 360 li from Ichang. Here the boat was made fast for the night. The weather had been fine during the day; thermometer 80°.

On April 2 got under way at 5 A.M. The weather was lovely, but the wind light and baffling, causing much hard work for the trackers and crew. A small rapid was passed during the day, and a gorge entered in which the boat was secured to the bank for the night. On shore I found a fine variety of wild rose, the flower being large and of a crimson colour. The scarcity of birds was remarkable. It was certainly nesting time, and they might be expected to be more in seclusion; but one rarely caught sight of a solitary specimen, with the exception of the small white heron, which is plentiful on the banks of the river. The Chinese do not destroy or trap them to any extent, and they do not appear to have many natural enemies.

On April 3 I got under way at 4.30 A.M. with a fair wind, and proceeded through the Wu-shan Gorge. This is the longest in the river, being twenty miles long. The hills here are about 2,000 feet high in places on each side, but breaking out here and there into more open country, and the scenery very fine, the land being cultivated where possible; but the population is sparse. The boat was made fast to the shore at the head of this gorge for the night, being now 560 li from Ichang and 1,400 from Chung-king. Several rapids

SCENE IN THE WU-SHAN GORGE.

were passed through during the day, none, however, being of any importance.

The next day the start was made at 4.30 A.M. to ascend the Fung-sien (wind-box) Gorge. Just before reaching the gorge the river takes a sharp turn, and there is a very awkward and dangerous rapid. Here the boat nearly came to serious grief through the carelessness of the *lowban* or captain. He did not use a stout enough tow rope or have enough trackers, the result being that the boat hung in the rapid, and then the rope carried away. A large junk was made fast to the bank, and her crew were asked to assist us, but they would not move a finger to help a foreign devil out of a most perilous situation.

The boat was driven back into a whirlpool, and by dint of hard work was huloed into a backwater and then to the bank, after having been swept down a considerable distance. This caused a vexatious delay, but upon proper precautions being now taken, the rapid was safely ascended and the gorge entered. It is very winding, and the scenery particularly striking. The mountains are high, and precipices are seen 2,000 feet deep. There are but few landing-places, and the locality is dark and gloomy. There are a number of Chinese coffins laid about in cracks and crevices that appear to be utterly inaccessible, and the wonder is how they were ever conveyed there. On the left bank a road has been blasted on the face of the precipice for about four miles, and is still in progress. Coolies may be seen suspended on the perpendicular face on plank scaffolds, drilling holes for the explosives. This is dangerous work, and I heard that many lives are lost.

The water is generally very deep and smooth, the current being strong. There are several rapids, but none of a dangerous character. At the head of the gorge the river takes a bend to the southward, and the banks break out very suddenly. There is a large sand-bank here that is uncovered when the river is low, and on which brine springs are found. This brine is evaporated in iron vessels, and a considerable quantity of salt is produced. Just above is Quei-chow-fu, which was reached at 6 P.M., and is 665 li from Ichang. It is a Le-kin station; and as now I had left the province of Hu-peh and was in Sze-chuen, the Custom House officials came on board and made a copy of my passport as the boat passed the town. I landed a few men to get provisions for the crew, and gave them orders to rejoin the boat further up the river. I had no intention of stopping off the place, as the men might get on shore, and then it is very uncertain when they would come off. The boat was made fast for the night just above the town.

This is a place of considerable importance, trading in salt and coal. Large junks come down from the upper parts of the river, but do not, as a rule, proceed lower down than this. Here I was obliged to take two soldiers on board as a guard. They go by the name of 'runners' among the Europeans, and are of little or no use when travelling by boat. On the road they are of great assistance in procuring lodgings. In the afternoon, before reaching the town, my dog Toby, a spaniel, jumped overboard, but could not land, and was carried two miles down the stream before he was picked up by a coolie whom I had sent down in a sampan to his assistance. This caused some delay.

April 5.—Started as usual at 4.30 A.M., and there being no wind the trackers had to go on shore. The current was very strong, and only fourteen li were got over during the day. The country passed through was open and highly cultivated, cereals, tobacco, and vegetables being largely grown.

April 6.—A welcome fair wind on starting, and at 9.30 came to a small rapid, which was safely got through. The wind helped us all day, and in the evening we got through a very bad rapid and then made fast for the night, having done 138 li—a very good run. Here I heard from the natives that there was a very bad place ahead. There is so little water near the banks in the river at this time of the year that it seems to be almost a series of rapids.

On April 7, the weather being bad, a start was not made till 7 o'clock, and I found three men missing, they having gone across the river without my leave or knowledge. The bad rapid I had heard of the night before was soon reached, and the water was boiling; with four men at the helm, and the bow sweep in use, it was almost impossible to steer the boat, and had it not been for a strong, fair wind I doubt if we should have got through. The banks are precipitous, with many sharp rocks and boulders, and altogether a dangerous place. Cedars and pines grow sparingly about among the rocks, and the scenery is fine, but dark and gloomy.

Near any rapid of importance a village is always to be found, the inhabitants making their living by tracking, and also by manufacturing and selling bamboo rope. They inhabit bamboo-framed huts so constructed as to be easily moved, and always live close to the water. When the river is low the huts are moved down as soon as the ground gets dry, and on its rising they are shifted back again.

On April 8 left at daylight with a fair wind, but not much of it. The vegetation seems to change about here, and I noticed a sort of banyan tree growing.

This is not the Indian species, as it sends down no adventitious roots from its branches, but is a handsome tree with foliage resembling laurel, and is very useful from the shade it affords.

All this part of Sze-chuen is very interesting, and is highly cultivated, with a fair population, principally engaged in farming. Anchored for the night just below Wan-hsien, a town on the left bank. On the opposite side are two conspicuous pagodas. The river here takes a big bend to the S.S.W., and according to my estimate is about a mile wide. The town is half-way between Ichang and Chung-king, and is a most picturesque place.

At Wan-hsien an English missionary came on board, and kindly offered to send any letters I might wish to dispatch down by the native post.

April 9.—Under way at daylight with a favourable but light wind, which soon died away. After having made sixty li the boat was secured to the shore opposite a small hamlet, no difficult places having been passed during the day.

April 10.—A start was made at daylight as usual, the day being fine, but no wind and a strong current made hard work for the trackers. It was very hot towards the middle of the day, and on landing I found some interesting species of plants, which I had not noticed as occurring lower down the river. These I collected and dried for future identification. The air was loaded with the perfume of orange blossoms, the fruit being largely cultivated about here, and forming an important article of commerce. The distance traversed to-day was only fifty li, and in the evening the boat was made fast just off a village.

April 11.—Weather still lovely; but as there was no wind it was hard work for the trackers, especially as the current was strong. The distance made was sixty li, and the boat was secured for the evening at the north end of what I believe to be the St. George's Island of Captain Gill. The bed of the river here is very rocky.

April 12.—Started against a strong current at daylight. This was a very close, steamy day, the thermometer being 80°, but the atmosphere oppressive. Mr. Kricheldorff fell overboard, but was picked up quickly, and suffered only from a thorough wetting. Fifty li were made to-day, and the boat was secured for the night off the village of Lung-chau, a small place all round which poppies are cultivated for the production of opium. This place is 600 li from Chung-king.

CHAPTER VII

JOURNEY UP THE RIVER CONTINUED

Necessity of haste—Intricacy of channel—Pagodas—Gold washers—Fu-chau—'Weigeren' boat—Meet Mr. George—Collecting larvæ and Coleoptera—Arrive at Chung-king—Visit Resident—A large and important town—Change in crews—Disagreeable incident—Leave Chung-king—Fine scenery—Bamboos and llamoo trees—Heronries—Vexatious delay—Cedars—Hostility at a small town—Poppies and tobacco—We land but are obliged to return—Robbery on board—Rise in river—Boat in danger—Man overboard—Lhu-chau in ruins—Meet Mrs. Riley—Arrive at Sui-fu—Beautiful place—Natives Mahommedan principally and well disposed to foreigners—Large trading place—Upper Yang-tze—Leave for Kia-ting-fu—Fishing with cormorants—Ancient caves—Chien-wei-hsien—Brine wells—Suicide of soldier—Chu-ken-tan.

April 13.—A light breeze helped us at our usual daylight start, and during the day I noticed the beauty of the vegetation, which was of a sub-tropical character. I often regretted that in such spots I could not make a longer stay; but knowing the importance of pushing on as rapidly as possible, for my intention was to get as far to the westward as I could before summer was too far advanced, I was obliged to forego the pleasure, in the hope that I might be able to make a stay on my return journey at those places which seemed the richest in natural history treasures. At noon the wind freshened and the poor trackers were somewhat relieved. The weather was cloudy, and a run of ninety-five li was made. The thermometer only showed 70° to-day, and in the evening the boat was secured near a small town about 505 li from Chung-king.

April 14.—The journey made to-day was much the same as usual; nothing of special note occurred, with the exception of the intricacy of the channel, to get safely through which I was obliged to engage a native pilot, there being so many dangerous rocks in the channel. Two pagodas were passed on the right bank of the river, and one on the left. The boat was made fast for the night, after having made a run of 100 li, about two miles above a small town on the right bank, the distance from Chung-king being now about 405 li.

April 15.—A light wind favoured us to-day, and eased the work of the trackers. The weather was cloudy but fine; thermometer 80°. There are no gorges in this part of the river, the country being more level. Flat sandbanks and shingle beds occur, and a good many men are engaged in washing for gold, which occurs rather more plentifully than lower down the river, but still in such small quantities as to make the industry profitable only to a Chinaman. Heaps of stones on the shingle banks formed by their washing operations are frequently seen. A run of sixty li was made to-day, and the distance from Chung-king is now reduced to 345 li. The country is well cultivated about here—cereals, pulse, tobacco, fruit, and poppies being grown. The district is well populated, and the inhabitants seem to be fairly well off.

April 16.—Started at daylight with a light favourable breeze, and passed Fu-chau at 4 P.M. Here the Khian river joins the Yang-tze-kiang, flowing down from the province of Quei-chau, which is one of the poorest and wildest in the Empire. Its rocky and rugged surface admits of but little cultivation, but it is probably rich in minerals. The halt for the night was made twenty li above Fu-chau.

On April 17 there was no wind at starting and a strong current. Only thirty-five li were made, and it rained in the evening.

April 18.—Heavy rain to-day. A head wind and current so strong that the trackers were unable to make way against it. At 4 P.M. the weather moderated, and a start was made. After proceeding slowly for half an hour, I was surprised by hearing a cry from my men of a 'weigeren' boat—that is to say, a boat containing an English man or men. On looking astern I saw a small boat flying a peculiar flag, which was evidently at first glance not Chinese. I stopped to allow it to overtake me, and on coming up found that it contained a Mr. George, of Streatham, who was travelling for a mercantile firm down the river. Hearing that Chung-king was about to be opened to English traders, he had come up with the intention of being first in the field if possible. At Ichang he had heard of my departure, and had pushed on with all speed hoping to overtake me, and we now travelled on in company. The thermometer to-day was 85°.

April 19.—A start was made at daylight this morning, and a beautiful country passed through, the vegetation being very rich. I collected a number of larvæ from the trunks of a species of poplar, and got a splendid series. They, unfortunately for me, were of the hairy species, and irritated the skin very much. I applied ammonia with a good result, but did not get much sleep at night. The worst of it was, that in changing to pupæ, all the hairs were shed and were blown about the cabin, getting into the sheets and every available spot, the consequence being that for some weeks we were liable to be stung. I also got some Coleoptera of the family Cicindela, an interesting class of sand beetle.

April 20.—Left with a light fair wind in the morning, and made fifty li, anchoring for the night forty li from Chung-king, which place I hope to reach tomorrow. The country now is getting more hilly, but not very interesting. Very few trees are seen. The thermometer 79° to-day, and rain fell in the evening.

April 21.—Arrived at Chung-king at noon. Took chairs on landing, as it was not wise for Europeans to walk in the streets at that time. A long and uncomfortable journey, taking nearly three quarters of an hour, principally up flights of steps, brought us to the house of Mr. Cockburn, the British Resident, who had passed nearly three years in this disagreeable place.

This is a very large and important city, being the principal centre for the Yunnan and Sze-chuen trade, many hundreds of junks trading from here as far down as Ichang and Sha-shih. It is a great place also for the distribution of foreign manufactured goods throughout these provinces.

At Chung-king a considerable change was made in my crew. I had among them some men who had been with me to Chang-yang, and whom I had trained as collectors. These I kept, as they would be again very useful, but the remainder, with the exception of the lowban, were discharged, and in their places men from Chung-king were engaged, as they were better acquainted with the upper parts of the river. These signed an agreement to take the boat to Kia-ting-fu in eighteen days, and in getting men, it is always necessary to have such a document prepared and signed by them, as they will be nearly sure to fail in their duty if merely verbally engaged.

A very disagreeable incident occurred here. I had offered one of my men a small sum each for the eggs of the white heron, and upon his bringing me a dozen I paid him what I had agreed. This did not suit him, and because I refused to be imposed upon, he threw the cash I had given him in my face. I was utterly powerless to retaliate in the slightest manner, as it would have caused a disturbance among the many boats close by, and probably my boat would have been looted and destroyed.

On April 24 I left Chung-king at 2 P.M., accompanied by Mr. Cockburn and Mr. George. This was an intensely hot day, the thermometer being at 100° in the boat. A short journey only of twenty-five li was made, when the boat was secured for the night.

April 25.—Started at 4.30 A.M. After having gone about four miles, Messrs. Cockburn and George left me to return to Chung-king in a sampan. They were the last Europeans seen by me, with the exception of my assistant and Mrs. Riley, until I arrived at Sui-fu, the town at the junction of the Min River with the Yang-tze-kiang. A little cooler to-day, the thermometer at 90° ; and fair progress made, ninety li.

April 26.—Left at daylight; the weather very fine but hot, and the scenery beautiful, the country being broken into ravines and valleys with lovely vegetation. No mountains are seen yet. Several villages were passed during the day, and the houses composing them seemed to be of better construction than those passed lower down. The boat was made fast to the bank for the night off a hamlet 150 li from Chung-king.

April 27.—Started at daylight, and at 8 A.M. passed a walled city on the left bank with a pagoda on the other side of the river nearly opposite. The scenery very fine about here. Clumps of graceful bamboos are mixed with small plantations of the llamoo, which is a very beautiful tree, having dark green foliage, a grey bark, and a tall but slender habit of growth. Though not growing to any great size, the wood is thought much of by the Chinese carpenter for small articles of furniture, boxes, &c., and it has a fragrant odour. The farmhouses are generally constructed under its shade, and it is used by the white heron, so common on the river, as a nesting-place. These birds have a similar habit to the common heron of this country, and form large heronries, the presence of which are thought by the Chinese to bring luck on the ground under which they are found.

A vexatious delay occurred now, two of the Chung-king men were reported to be sick, and all the remainder wanted to return to take them back. Now this would have caused a serious delay, and besides, have put me to a considerable loss, for they had all been paid half their wages to Kia-ting-fu. My lowban, however, here showed himself to be captain of the boat by deeds and not in name only, for after some considerable talk he managed to fasten upon the originator of the trouble, and seizing him by the pigtail, he gave him a sound thrashing with a bamboo, which at once cured him of his sickness and rendered him fit for work again. This was, no doubt, a rather dangerous method of governing the crew in a district so far from any hope of help in case of downright mutiny, but it answered, I am glad to say, perfectly, and I had no further trouble with the men on this score.

The character of the vegetation changed to-day, and many trees of the cedar species were seen, together with the sweet chestnut. Eighty li were made, and the weather was slightly cooler; thermometer 85°.

April 28.—Made a start at dawn as usual, and during the day a small town was passed, from which crowds of people came down to the banks and stoned the boat, crying out, 'Kill the foreign devils.'

Many stones pitched on board, but luckily no serious damage was done. This was the first instance of my having received anything but civility from the inhabitants of Sze-chuen, except at the town of Chung-king. Enormous fields of poppies are passed through about here, which are grown for the production of opium. Tobacco is also largely grown, and of two sorts. The boat was anchored for the night at a small place called Lung-chi, after having made eighty li during the day. The atmosphere was very oppressive during the night and I fully expected a thunderstorm, but none came. These are frequent, and seem to follow the course of the river to a great extent.

April 29.—Started at dawn with a fair wind which soon headed us, and after having made twenty-four li, we were obliged to anchor for two hours. On proceeding, we passed through two rapids, one being rather bad, and in the afternoon heavy rain came down.

On anchoring I went ashore with Mr. Kricheldorff to search for larvæ, or what else we might chance to find, but the threatening attitude of the mob soon forced us to retire to the boat without having found anything to speak of. The progress made to-day was sixty li.

April 30—Left at daylight, and soon after the start found that a thief had been on board during the night. Some of the lowban's things were taken, and also some of Mr. Kricheldorff's. These latter had been hooked off from pegs, through a window on the opposite side of the cabin, this being the only possible means by which they could have been abstracted. During the night I had been awakened by hearing the dog growl, but noticing no further sound went to sleep again. These boat-thieves are fairly common on the river, and usually are most expert swimmers and divers. If they are discovered, they go overboard at once, and being quite unencumbered with clothing, are able to make the best use of their proficiency in the water. The low-ban got some of his things on going back to the village, but none of Mr. Kricheldorff's were recovered. A pagoda was passed during the day, near which was a very bad rapid, one of two we had to ascend. The river is rising and much discoloured, this being probably caused by heavy rain to the westward, as from all I have heard it is yet much too early for the general rise caused by the melting of the snow.

May 1.—A rise of from 6 to 8 feet had taken place in the river during the night. On starting, the boat was taken over to the other side, and on looking out I found her already in a rapid, and in a most dangerous place. Before many minutes we were on a rock forming part of a ledge jutting out into the river. Just before striking it, one of my strongest men fell overboard through the ironshod bamboo pole, which he was trying to fend off with, slipping on the face of the

BOAT IN A RAPID, SHOWING BOW SWEEP READY FOR USE.

stone. In a moment he was carried far astern. He was a good swimmer, and after half an hour's struggle managed to reach the shore—a miraculous escape. Many sampans were about, but not one would put off to render him the slightest assistance. There were fifty-two trackers on the tow rope besides my own men, and their deliberate refusal to exert themselves was the cause of the boat getting into this perilous position. I have no doubt it was a plot among them to wreck her, either from ill-feeling or from the hope of being able to steal the wreckage. After half an hour the current took us off, having swept the boat clear, and then after getting outside again, the ascent was safely made. My men now landed, and though they were in such small numbers, attacked the natives and inflicted a severe chastisement, not, however, without receiving some heavy blows in return. These trackers, I should mention, were not paid a single cash. I went down to the place where the man was who had fallen overboard, taking some whisky with me. I found him rather weak and exhausted, but he returned on board with me, and was all right the next day. Unless he had been such a powerful man he must have been drowned.

While the boat was fast on the rock, the body of a man was washed down the river, a poor tracker, I should say, for he had what I took to be a tracking-belt round him. I called the lowban's attention to it, but he refused to look at the body. The boat was anchored off a small village at the end of this exciting day, after having made sixty-four li.

May 2.—Started at daylight with a slight breeze: soon after I went on shore with Mr. Kricheldorff. The scenery here is very beautiful, there being many of the groves of llamoo trees mentioned before. To-day the city of Lu-chau was passed and was a sad sight, as twenty days ago two-thirds of the city had been burnt, and now presented a dismal spectacle of bare and blackened walls. Official assistance had to be rendered to save many of the inhabitants from starvation. It was a city of perhaps 100,000 inhabitants, situated on the left bank of the Yang-tze, just above the junction of the Choong River.

May 3.—After proceeding about ten li to-day, a junk was met, with a Mrs. Riley, the widow of a missionary, and her three children on board. She was travelling down from Cheng-tu, and had had some Europeans with her as far as Sui-fu, but was now by herself, and on the way to Ichang. It was cooler to-day, the thermometer being at 70°, and fifty li were made.

May 4.—Nothing of note occurred to-day, except that I noticed a large species of bamboo which more resembled the tropical types. It rained hard all day and seventy-five li were made.

May 5.—Beautiful scenery was passed through to-day, the country being undulating. At mid-day a small city was passed, of a different and more graceful style of architecture than those seen below.

On May 6 a distance of sixty li was made, and Sui-fu was reached on the following day at 8.30 A.M. This is the Soo-Chau of Blakiston, and is situated on the right bank of the Min River at its confluence with the Yang-tze. It is built on high ground, and trees growing from the banks of the river up to the city walls make it a strikingly beautiful place, the waters of the two rivers washing the base of the eminence on which it stands. The population is composed largely of Mahommedans, and they are particularly civil to Europeans. The town is very clean, with good shops, and there is a special wharf for the trade with Yunnan, which is large, the border of the province being within a comparatively short distance. Here, among other things, may be seen bales of the skins of wild beasts, such as bears, leopards, tigers, deer, badgers, and wolves.

I had no trouble here with my passport, and met two missionaries, Messrs. Wellwood and Owen, on a visit from Cheng-tu, from which town they had accompanied Mrs. Riley on her journey down the river. The population of the town is considerable, there being 64,000 registered houses. There is a very picturesque temple on the opposite bank of the Min River, built in a grove of trees. A very bad rapid was reported to exist just above the town, but from what I heard, I hoped to reach Kia-ting-fu in seven days.

At no considerable distance up the Yang-tze above Sui-fu is Ping-shan, beyond which I was informed the river is not considered to be navigable. Very deep and narrow gorges are found, and the rapids are impassable. Small local boats and sampans ply between them, but nothing except timber rafts attempt to pass down. Very little is known about this part of the river, and the navigation of these rafts is considered to be so dangerous that it is a regular part of the contract for the crews to be provided with their coffins. Ping-shan is also an outpost of the Imperial troops, who have constant trouble with the Lolos.

On May 8 a start was made from Sui-fu, the boat being towed by seventy coolies through the long rapid just above the town. The towing path was on the left bank, and I saw for the first time fishing cormorants used. Unfortunately they were some distance away, but they were perfectly tame and well under command, being used from long bamboo rafts, each raft having about six birds. I went on shore during the day and saw some particularly interesting caves cut in the red sandstone. In many of these Chinese coffins had been deposited, and in one, where the coffin had been placed near the mouth, it was nearly covered with the roots of a tree which were as large round as a man's body. These caves were made for dwellings by a race which inhabited the country before the Chinese drove them out, and are probably very ancient. Some are of considerable extent, and the marks of the gouge or tool with which the inside was finished may still be seen in most of them. Many are on the faces of precipices some distance up, and could only be reached by ladders laid up to landing-places. They appear to be dry and have couches or bed places, still to be seen, cut in the sandstone.

May 9.—The waters still very strong, and plenty of trackers required. After travelling ninety li the boat was made fast off a village where there was an iron-foundry for casting pans or boilers for use at the brine wells further up the river.

May 10.—Hard work for the trackers against the strong current. The sail is never used in these upper parts of the river though the mast is kept stepped, as it is often necessary to have the towing rope from the mast-head. The vegetation is much varied here, and in the cultivated ground, cereals, tobacco, and poppies may be seen. Peaches and apricots are also grown, but these are always gathered and eaten green by the Chinese, Europeans seldom getting an opportunity of procuring them ripe.

May 11.—Sixty li were made to-day against a strong current as usual, but no rapids were passed. The scenery was beautiful and the character of the country changing, becoming more mountainous. The boat was secured off Chien-wei-hsien.

May 12.—The scenery became more wild to-day, and the country was less cultivated. A long and bad rapid called Chayi-tai was passed through. It took four hours' hard work, and is, at the present state of the river, a dangerous place. Just above the river divides and an island is formed.

May 13.—Passed through lovely scenery to-day, but still with little cultivated ground. The chief industry here is the production of salt by boiling brine, which is found in wells, many of which are sunk to a considerable depth, most being on the left bank of the river. To-day I had the misfortune to lose one of the soldiers sent as a guard from Quei-chow-fu. They were constantly in the habit, when a short distance from a town, of landing and completing the journey on foot, rejoining me on arrival. Consequently their absence from the boat was thought nothing of; but this time the only news I had of the missing man was that he had been found quite dead, with no marks of violence, in a small pool by the river, and in which there was between two and three feet of water only. From what I heard, and from the circumstances under which the body was found, I am of the opinion that it was a case of suicide, but for what reason I am unable to conjecture. No inquiry was made into the matter, and I heard nothing further about it. The boat was secured for the night off the town of Chu-ken-tan, which is considered to be the centre of the salt trade. The country about this place is much more thickly populated than the districts I have lately passed through. I was now only forty-five li from Kia-ting-fu.

CHAPTER VIII

KIA-TING-FU TO WA-SHAN

Arrival at Kia-ting-fu—Attack by students—Stone throwing—Retreat to a safe position—Message from Tao-tai—Am prisoner in boat—Prepare for overland journey—Assistance from missionaries—Instructions to lowban—Adopt Chinese dress—Colossal image—Visit from Tao-tai—Reports about boat—Explanations—Difficulty as to route—Leave for Wa-shan—Su-chi—*Dendrobium* seen—Omêi-hsien—Wax insect, how made use of—Yang-tsun—Hsin-chang—Robbers outside inn—Lolo houses—Dangerous paths—'Times' of 1877 at Lulu-ping—Tung River—Antelopes at Chin-kou-ho—Arrive at Ta-tien-chih—Père Martin—Wild animals and birds in district—Fruits and flowers—Trip to base of Wa-shan—View—Icicles—Tributary Lolos—Collections—Arrival of mail—Description of Mount Wa.

May 14.—After a very rainy night a start was made early in the morning, tracking as usual against a strong current. Kia-ting-fu was reached at 3.30 P.M., and the boat made fast close to the city. Before long, however, a shower of stones astonished us, and the crew set to work to get the boat under way again in the hope of getting to a safer place. This was a matter of no slight danger, and several of my men were injured by the stones, many of which, as large as big apples, fell into the boat. The men, however, stuck to their work, and the boat drifting down the river was followed by the rapidly increasing mob who got out on a spit of shingle and continued the stone throwing. The water was very shallow and the boat touched several times but was happily got off again, for if she had become fixed we should possibly all have been either severely hurt or massacred. At last we got beyond their reach, and when at a safe distance away, the boat was secured. My passport was examined and the Tao-tai sent a message requesting me not to approach the town, as the triennial examinations were going on, and ten thousand students had come in for examination. I also heard that the two resident missionaries had left the town, as it was nearly always in a disturbed state at such a time.

I was, however, a prisoner in my boat until such time as the students might disperse, their work being over, but I was able to make preparations for the overland journey to Wa-shan, the river no longer being of service to me in the direction I wished to proceed, by looking over the various things I wished to take, and getting them packed into loads for coolies and weighing them. In this I was assisted by Messrs. Ririe and Vale of the China inland mission, to whom I had sent a coolie informing them of my arrival. It is essential that the loads should be as nearly equal in weight as possible, or there is nearly sure to be discontent among the carriers.

I had with me a man from Chung-king, engaged at the recommendation of the Consul, who gave him the character of being a reliable fellow, and to him fell the duty of going to the coolie hong and sending the manager to me. With him I entered into the usual agreement as to price, he being responsible for the honesty of the coolies he was to provide and also for the head men over them. The remainder of the Chung-king men were discharged and sent home, this leaving me with five men and the captain. Three of these were competent collectors, having been under my tuition at Chang-yang, and they now had orders to make collections in the neighbourhood, and especially at the place where I intended to leave the boat, which was on the opposite bank to, and about a mile below, the city, close to a hill covered with pine trees beneath the shade of which several temples had been built, one of which contained a great many gilt images. The lowban was left in charge of the boat, a place of responsibility, as on the first indications of a flood he had to take the boat to the other side and have her secured in a back-water. He also had orders to scrape the boat, as I found that the white colour she was painted attracted a great deal of attention, and then varnish her in the same way that all the native boats are done.

The floods here are no trifles, and the level of the

SCENE ON MIN RIVER NEAR KIA-TING FU.

river may perhaps rise many feet in a night, the only indications being a slight discolouration a few hours before. They are occasioned by the melting of the snow in the mountains.

Mr. Kricheldorff and I now had our heads shaved, and got into Chinese clothes, including an artificial tail which was secured inside the cap. These we found to be very cool and comfortable, but the chief advantage we gained was, that when so dressed, little or no attention was paid to us by the mob.

I was unable to visit the town at all on this occasion for the reason stated before, and am therefore unable to say anything about it. On the opposite side of the river there is a colossal image cut out of the red sandstone. It is seated, with the hands on the knees, and must be at least 150 feet high. The head is overgrown with creepers, and small trees have taken root and are growing. These will, in course of time, utterly destroy the work, but as yet the outline can be distinctly traced.

Two days before I intended to leave, the Tao-tai came down with his staff of about fifteen attendants, all most richly dressed, himself in particular wearing a navy blue satin tunic, covered with the most beautiful embroidery in different coloured silks. There was not room for all, but he came on board and informed me that it was reported that I had an infernal machine, and that my intention was to destroy the city. I tried to assure him that such was not the case, and eventually succeeded in convincing him that my object was only the collecting of objects interesting to naturalists, such as birds, butterflies, &c. He could not or would not understand, and asked what good could they be, and what was I going to do with them. I said that I had a passport for the province and intended to go to Wa-shan for the purpose, when after I had made such collections as I could, they would be sent home to people who were greatly interested in such things, and who would highly appreciate them.

He then appeared to be to a certain extent satisfied, but said he could not give me a guard to Wa-shan, or allow me to proceed there, and from what I could gather he wished me to go in the direction of Cheng-tu. This I refused to assent to, and said that my destination was Wa-shan, and that I intended to go there whether I had his permission or not, as I had a perfect right to travel in any part of Sze-chuen. After some further conversation he left, apparently not in a good temper. My object, however, was gained, for just before I left, he sent a guard of two men to accompany me as far as Omêi-hsien, where they would be relieved and fresh ones sent on. I found out that his reluctance to allow me to travel by the route I had chosen arose from the fact that it passed close to the frontier of the Lolos, who are an independent tribe, or rather race, with whom the Chinese Government are constantly in a state of war, and whom they had never been able to subdue. He feared that in one of the raids which they frequently make I might be taken prisoner, and then he would be held responsible.

On May 19, having got thirty coolies for my loads, a start was made at 10 A.M. for Wa-shan, where I intended to stay the whole of the summer, and return to the boat in the autumn, run down the river to Ichang and send my collections home. Besides the coolies, I had Mr. Kricheldorff, the two soldiers as a guard, and an interpreter with me. It was a soaking wet day, and my halting-place, a small market town called Su-chi, was reached at 4 P.M. The footpaths are narrow and the country passed through of a red sandstone formation. Four branches of rivers were crossed, and this caused some delay. I found an indifferent inn and was able to purchase some eggs, and felt a sense of relief now that Kia-ting-fu, where I was forced to remain in my boat, was left behind.

May 20.—Left Su-chi at 6.30, passing through a lovely country reminding me of Hampshire. It is very fertile, and water wheels of large diameter, fitted with bamboo cups, are used for irrigating. During the day I saw a large clump of *Dendrobium nobile* in bloom, growing about ten feet from the ground on a species of ash tree. I reached Omêi-hsien in the evening, and here my passport was copied. The guard was changed also, two fresh soldiers being sent from the Yamen. Mount Omêi, 11,100 feet high, is twenty li from here and is a magnificent solitary peak. I could not ascend it on this journey, but intend to do so when I return.

May 21.—The country is still lovely; weather cloudy. Chinese coolies were passed carrying the eggs of the wax insect to the eastward.

These curious insects, which are a species of *coccus*, are bred on one kind of tree, but are transported about 200 miles to produce the wax, which they do upon a totally different species of tree to that upon which they are bred.

They are produced principally in the valley of the Anning river, a tributary of the Ya-lung, and I gathered from inquiries that the eggs appear in large numbers in the month of March upon the branches of the large-leaved privet (*Ligustrum lucidum*), being enclosed in small pear-shaped excrescences or scales.

The scales are gathered at the end of April, and made up in paper packets weighing about 16 oz. each. About sixty of these form a coolie's load, and during transit great care is taken of them, the coolie travelling only by night or on dull days, as the sunlight matures the contents of the scales too rapidly. At the resting places the loads are unpacked, and the packets spread thinly in cool and shady places. Most of the coolies travel by way of Fulin, at which place they cross the Tung River, but I was informed that some make a more direct route by crossing the country of the independent Lolos, who permit them to do so on payment of duty.

They reach Kia-ting-fu about the beginning of May, when the small packets are undone and from twenty to thirty scales are enclosed in a leaf of the wood oil tree (*Aleurites cordata*) in which some rough holes are made to allow of the escape of the insects and also to pass pieces of rice straw through, by means of which it is attached to the branch of the tree upon which the wax is produced. This is a species of ash (*Fraxinus chinensis*), which is grown, in a pollard form, in great quantities round the edges of the rice fields, and up to the foot of the mountains in the district around Kia-ting-fu.

In fine weather the insects soon creep out of the scales and up the branches on to the twigs, on the under side of which the wax soon begins to appear. This gradually increases, coating the twig or branch all over, and in about a hundred days has attained a thickness of perhaps a quarter of an inch.

The branches are then lopped off, and as much as possible of the wax is carefully scraped off and thrown into boiling water, from which it is skimmed as it rises to the surface. This is the best wax. The branches and twigs are then thrown into the pot, but the wax melted from them is darker and inferior.

It is used for making candles or coating those made from inferior substance, and for giving a polish to wood-work, &c.

Yang-tsun was reached at 4 P.M. and a halt made for the night, having travelled seventy li.

May 22.—Started at 6.30, and, travelling through a very fertile valley, the small village of Lung-chi was reached at 9.30. From here the road ascends, and Hsin-chang was reached in the afternoon. I had a very bad room in the inn, but was very tired and had to put up with it. It was between two cesspools.

The village inns are generally built of mud and in the form of a square, with rooms built facing inwards from the outside wall. In the centre is a court which is sometimes paved, and in the middle of the court is generally a depression or hole which is the receptacle for all sorts of filth. As a rule the inns are dirty in the extreme, especially when the village is not on a high road, and sometimes, but rarely, a room is found in them better and cleaner than the rest, probably reserved for an official when travelling. During the night a cry of thieves was raised, and about a dozen were seen outside the gates. I had twenty-two men with me, the remainder being at another inn, and no attack was made. They left as the day was breaking, after having stayed for nearly five hours. I was glad to find no reinforcements come up, and had an anxious time, having a good deal of silver with me, a fact they were probably aware of.

May 23.—Left at 7 A.M. and crossed a tributary of the Tung River at 9 o'clock, travelling through a very wild and rugged region. Lolo houses could be seen on the other side of the valley of the Tung River. These houses can be easily distinguished from those of the Chinese, being built of stone instead of mud, and having flat roofs, small windows, and watch towers. The path now is very narrow and dangerous; a slip might send one rolling down hundreds of feet.

After a tiring day got to Lulu-ping at 4 P.M. This place is at an elevation of 4,250 feet. I found the landlord of the inn very civil. He showed me a part of the weekly 'Times' of November 23, 1877, containing a report of part of the celebrated trial of Benson and others. This newspaper had been left behind by Mr.

Baber on his way to Wa-shan eleven years ago. The landlord also informed me that no European had passed since. During the day, which was very wet, I saw some feathers of the Amherst pheasant lying about on the path.

May 24.—The main stream of the Tung was struck to-day. The road, or rather path, was dreadful, being very narrow, and winding about on deep declivities, often with a precipice on one side where a fall would be fatal, and barely room to crawl along in single file.

At places the Tung might be seen tearing along its rocky bed hundreds of feet below. This is the wildest region I have yet been in, and the river forms practically the boundary between the Chinese and the Lolos. I arrived at Chin-kou-ho at 3 P.M. This village is situated in a ravine, and has a roaring torrent running beside it, the opposite bank of the stream being formed by a precipice. Found a very bad inn here, and had a room given me over a cesspool. Finding the stench unbearable, I made an exchange with the soldiers sent from the Yamen, they not appearing to object in the slightest. During the day I found several interesting species of Lepidoptera, and from what I could judge this hot, steamy gorge should prove a good spot for collecting, and I shall note it as a station for some of my men by and by. At about 4 P.M. I saw from the window of my room several antelopes on a narrow ledge of the precipice, and hardly twenty yards away. My rifle was unfortunately with the coolies in the other inn, but I immediately hurried after it, and succeeded in getting a shot which secured one. This caused great excitement in the village, and two men swam across to fetch it. It was very lucky, and gave us a supply of meat for a couple of days, making a most agreeable change in our diet from the everlasting rice, Indian corn cakes and eggs, with sometimes, but not often, a fowl.

May 25.—Left at 6 A.M. The road led to the east of a spur, and was partly on the bank of a tributary of the Tung River, through the villages of Nan-mu-yuan and Li-mien-tien, and took me to Kuei-hua-chang, where I stayed the night, being now only fifteen li from my destination at Ta-tien-chih. The weather was cloudy, and a mountainous region was passed through with very trying paths.

May 26.—Left at 7 A.M., and arrived at Ta-tien-chih at 11. Here I found Père Joseph Martin on a visit to his converts, his headquarters being at Huang-mu-chang about seventy li further on. He had not seen a European since Baber, eleven years ago, and was kind enough to lend me the old mission house to live in. I appreciated this very much, as it was greatly superior to any other house in the village, and very comfortable. This devoted man has lived in the neighbourhood for many years, and has no intention of ever returning to Europe. He has made many converts, and is much beloved by them. There is a good chapel at Huang-mu-chang, and when he is visiting outlying districts he holds services in the houses of the natives. I noticed for the first time some joss houses that had been allowed to fall to ruins.

As soon as my things had been got into the house, I paid off and dismissed the coolies, keeping only four with me, as I intended to remain here all the summer.

I should mention that the mission house, the use of which was so kindly granted me, was situated on the side of a hill, and was facing Mount Wa, which towered 6,000 feet above us.

The day after my arrival I started to see what could be done in the way of collecting, and ascending the slopes of a hill opposite, a spur from the mountain, I got into a terribly bad road, very stony and precipitous, and much overgrown with jungle in places. Old watercourses had to be traversed. I found many interesting plants, which I collected to be dried, but came to the conclusion that it was too early and cold yet for butterflies. It was bad getting up, but much worse getting down.

MISSION-HOUSE, TA-TIEN-CHIH, AT THE FOOT OF MOUNT WA.

The country appears to be thinly inhabited, and I noticed a change in the headgear worn, for here the hat, instead of being small, is made of two thicknesses of heavy felt, the inside being of a light colour and the outer black, or nearly so, the brim being much turned up. I found that this shape is peculiar to Western China and Eastern Tibet, where it is exclusively worn. Indian corn is grown and also potatoes, which have been introduced by the French missionaries. There is not, however, much cultivated ground, the country generally being thickly wooded, the surface rugged, and in places large, steep, detached hills, with sides partly precipitous, are found. The long and graceful bamboo is not seen, its place being taken by a shorter and more scrubby variety. I was told that tigers, leopards, bears, and antelope abounded, and also that the wild ox, which I suppose to be the Budorcas of Père David, is found on the slopes at the base of Mount Wa. The only part of one of these that I was fortunate enough to see was a piece of the hide. They are reputed to be very active and fierce, and are hunted in the winter by the Lolos for the sake of their flesh, which makes good beef. They are of a grey colour, with horns large and spreading, meeting at the base and turned back at the point. The tragopan is fairly plentiful, and the beautiful Amherst pheasant is common.

Two pairs of these were brought to me alive, having been snared by the leg, and I purchased them for 1,000 cash, or about three shillings. There are also two species of pigeons resembling the blue rock, and living among the cliffs. Of the smaller species I shot several for food, but the larger variety was much more wild and difficult to get near. The district appears to be rich in botanical treasures. Quantities of fine wild strawberries were brought in by the boys at times; so many, in fact, that my cook made jam of them. Two sorts of raspberries and gooseberries are also found growing wild, and were often brought to the mission house. Very beautiful wild roses grew, the most remarkable being with a dark red bloom.

Towards the end of May the weather was very changeable, with a good deal of rain, and sometimes it was very cold, much the same sort of climate as I found at Chang-yang at the same time last year. The four seasons are more clearly marked than in the lower parts of China.

June 10 being a fine warm day, almost the first that we had had, I ascended the first base, if I may so call it, of Mount Wa, and on proceeding to examine its southern slopes I found them covered with virgin forest. The weather had been cold, and no butterflies to speak of were seen; it was too early for them. It being a clear day, the great Snowy Mountains above Ta-tsien-lu could be plainly seen to the north-west. They are eighty miles away as the crow flies, and the journey there takes eight or nine days from Ta-tien-chih. Far up the mountain in the crevices and hanging from projections on the rocks, huge icicles could be seen with the aid of a glass. These, it is no exaggeration to say, were in many cases as large as a church steeple, and when they fall they bring down tons of earth and rock with them, leaving huge semicircular cavities in the places from which they have been suspended.

On June 15 some Lolos paid us a visit. These were not the independent but tributary or subject Lolos, and are allowed to travel and work in China on the borders of their own country. They are not allowed to wear the horn, the distinctive mark of a true Lolo, and which is formed by the hair being knotted above the forehead, and then wrapped in a cloth, to form a projection some inches in length, but had on small flat Chinese caps. They are very different in appearance from the Chinese, and evidently a distinct race. Their height is about the average, and they are strong, active, wiry, and splendid mountaineers. A few carried matchlocks, the remainder spears about ten feet long, and they had with them a pack of hounds, miserable-looking specimens. They told me that they hunted the wild cattle, and that in the neighbourhood were two species of bear, two species of antelope, wolves, &c., all of which they pursued, but more principally in the autumn and winter. They were very poorly equipped for such sport I thought. They are looked down upon by the independent Lolos, who are a most interesting race, about which very little is known, no one as yet having been able to penetrate into the country. The weather now was a little warmer, and butterflies more numerous. I captured many rare and interesting species. In spare time I used to shoot a few pigeons to vary my diet, which consisted principally of Indian corn cake and eggs. I had a few tins of provisions with me, but considered them luxuries. I was lucky enough also to find plenty of watercress growing in a brook flowing through the limestone, and it made a welcome addition to my table.

On June 16, as the weather appeared to have set in fine and warm, I commenced night work, and was able by sugaring to obtain rare noctuæ.

While I was at Kia-ting-fu I made arrangements with the missionaries there—Messrs. Ririe and Vale—to have my mails sent to their care, and having sent a coolie in from this place to inquire, he returned on June 17, bringing letters and newspapers, which gave me some idea of what was going on in the civilised world. The mails, as far as Kia-ting-fu, are forwarded by the Chinese post, but the dates of their arrivals are very uncertain.

I took several photographs while at this place, one of the mission house being here reproduced. I also took one of Mount Wa, which unfortunately got spoiled by the light getting to it. I regretted this very much, as it is such a peculiarly shaped and interesting mountain. It has been so well described by Mr. Baber in his valuable book that I cannot do better than quote from it. 'The upper story of this most imposing mountain is a series of twelve or fourteen precipices rising one above another, each not much less than 200 feet high, and receding very slightly on all four sides from the one next below it. Every individual precipice is regularly continued all round the four sides. Or it may be considered as a flight of thirteen steps, each 180 feet high and thirty feet broad. Or, again, it may be described as thirteen layers of square, or slightly oblong, limestone slabs, 180 feet thick and about a mile on each side, piled with careful regularity and exact levelling upon a base 8,000 feet high. Or perhaps it may be compared to a cubic crystal stuck amid a row of irregular gems. Or perhaps it is beyond compare.'

CHAPTER IX

WA-SHAN TO TA-TSIEN-LU

Decide to visit Ta-tsien-lu—Preparations for journey—Coolies' loads—So-i-ling Pass—Huang-mu-chang—Père Martin—Chin-ki-za—Fu-lin—Its trade and produce—Inhospitality—Trouble about horses and coolies—Procure mules but lose them at Ni-tou—Fei-yueh-ling Pass—Pines and rhododendrons—Magnificent view—Dirt and discomfort at Leng-chi—Valley of the Tung River—Suspension bridge at Lu-ting-chiao—Cha-pa—Welcomed by missionaries—A flood in a watercourse—Bad road—Ruined houses—The Tung in flood—Traffic on the road—Fruit at Wa-ssu—Road to Ta-tsien-lu—Zones of vegetation—Single rope bridge—Arrival at Ta-tsien-lu—Kindness of Bishop Biet.

My collectors were now well up to their duties, and quite able, I thought, to complete such work as might be done here without my personal supervision. I therefore decided upon changing my original plan of stopping here all the summer and, leaving them and the collections already made behind, to advance to Ta-tsien-lu. The botanical collector was left in charge, and I found that thirty men were to be put under him, these being told off for such stations as I considered most promising.

On June 25 my last preparations were made by sending letters down to Kia-ting-fu, and packing up all that might be necessary. Finding that there was nothing to prevent my going, and as I was particularly anxious not to lose more of the season than was absolutely necessary, there being a species of butterfly (*Parnassius Imperator*) found further west, a series of which I wished to secure, I made a start on the following day with Mr. Kricheldorff, my cook and interpreter, and six coolies. These coolies carry enormous loads, considering the mountainous nature of the country and the rough roads they have to travel over, to say nothing of the poor nature of the food they have to live upon. From Kia-ting-fu to Wa-shan their loads were supposed to be as nearly sixty catties as possible each, but I found that from Wa-shan to Ta-tsien-lu the custom was for them to carry eighty catties, a catty being as nearly as possible one pound and a third. The road ascends for about four hours' march, passing through forest, the ground being very rocky and the path winding. At last the summit of the So-i-ling Pass is reached, which is 8,778 feet above the sea level. After descending some distance by a particularly tortuous road a very deep wild ravine is suddenly seen. The path leads along the southern side for about four miles, when there is an abrupt descent, and the neck of the ravine is crossed by a stone bridge. Then after a steep ascent the road leads along the opposite side of the ravine to nearly the point on the other side to which it entered. This is only mentioned to show what a long distance has to be traversed in many cases when the actual advance is very small. I saw several young wild pigs during the day, but no old ones.

Huang-mu-chang was my halting place for the night, when I again met Père Martin and had a hearty welcome from him and an invitation to stay at his house. He has a nice place with a good garden, in which are many familiar flowers, such as sweet william, cockscombs, and many other things, the seeds of which have been sent him from France. In the kitchen garden also he has vegetables, such as we are accustomed to at home, and is gradually spreading the cultivation of such of them as thrive well among the Chinese.

I parted from Père Martin the next morning (June 27) at 9 o'clock, and travelling as usual through a very mountainous region reached a market village called Chin-ki-za at 5.30 P.M., having walked sixty li from Huang-mu-chang. This was a very hard day's work, the roads as usual being very bad, and I think that the poorness of the food upon which we had lived was beginning to tell upon Mr. Kricheldorff and myself. At this place the soldiers or runners left me in order to report themselves at the Yamen of Ching-chi-hsien, from which place their successors were to be sent on to me.

June 28.—Made a start at 6 A.M. The road descended all the morning until Fu-lin was entered at noon. This is a curiously situated place, being built upon a low-lying plateau close to the Tung River. Several streams join it here, and between them are high barren ranges of hills, the plateau in its lowest parts bearing the most unmistakable signs of being frequently flooded, as it is covered with water-worn pebbles.

Fu-lin is an important place, and does a considerable trade in wheat, barley, Indian corn, and millet. Flour of excellent quality is produced, and very fine pears are grown, suitable only for cooking purposes. Apples and peaches, bringalls and potatoes, are also sold here in large quantities. The town is very thickly populated and the inhabitants most inhospitable. I was unfortunately without my guard, and in consequence I was not even allowed to sit down and rest in the town at an inn, so there was nothing but to march through and have our midday halt and meal under a tree outside the boundary. It is a very hot place, having high hills to the north. Arrived at Tang-chia-pa at 6 P.M. and tried to hire horses to carry us to Ta-tsien-lu, as the marching over such rough roads was getting too severe. These having been promised, I dismissed the coolies from Wa-shan also, as I was informed that I could replace them here.

June 29.—While we were at breakfast the Chinese horse owner brought the horses round, and was told to wait. He did so for a time, and then took the horses away, having no doubt been threatened with violence if he let his horses to the foreign devils. This put me in a nice fix, for the coolies dismissed the evening before had gone back, and I had loads to be transported when neither horses nor coolies were to be hired. At last I sent a message to the headman by my interpreter, saying that if horses and coolies were not provided forthwith I should send to Ching-chi-hsien and report him for having caused me delay. This message had the desired effect, but not wholly, for I got coolies but no horses. These, however, enabled me to leave the place, and after going about ten li a man with mules was met and an agreement made with him to take us on to Ta-tsien-lu. The mules had no saddles, but he said he could procure them at Ni-tou, and so we had to make shift with blankets. The road all day led by the side of a river bed or watercourse now nearly dry, but showing unmistakable signs that at times there must be heavy floods. It was a barren country with rocks and boulders of red sandstone. Heavy rain fell in the afternoon, and I was heartily glad when a small place was reached, twenty-five li from Ni-tou, where we could sleep.

June 30.—A start being made at 6 A.M., Ni-tou was reached at noon. Here the owner of the mules reported that the animals wanted shoeing, but, after a reasonable time had been allowed, they were not forthcoming. Truly the Chinese are a most vexatious people to deal with. All these little troubles arose through my not having the soldiers with me, but I certainly had expected them to have met me before this. There was nothing for it but to proceed on foot, and be thankful that I had at least some coolies to carry my baggage. I reached a small place ten li beyond San-chuo-ping at 4 P.M., and stopped there for the night, as there were no houses on the road between this and Hua-ling-ping, which was too far off to be reached.

July 1.—Started at 6 A.M. The road was ascending now as the Fei-yueh-ling Pass was being approached. This is at an elevation of 9,020 feet, and the ascent is hard work, the roads as usual being very bad. The principal trees are pines mingled with other evergreens, and in the open spaces several species of *Hydrangea* are seen. Higher up rhododendrons and azaleas flourish, some of the former being still in bloom, one being conspicuous from the fine deep carmine colour of its flower.

I took here some fine specimens of an interesting form of 'Apatura.' Near the summit, from which there is a fine view, the road leads in a semicircle round a deep ravine or bay several miles across, and the forest is looked down upon. This, with the clouds rolling beneath, presents a remarkable spectacle. The temperature was cool and a welcome change from the stifling heat of the valleys. We now descended to Leng-chi, where we arrived in an exhausted state, and tumbled into the first inn that presented itself. In justice to the town I may here say that if we had gone a little further we might have had more decent accommodation, for though I had some idea of what a dirty place a Chinese inn might be, this one for filth, discomfort, and the quantity of vermin that it contained was entitled to take the cake. My room was small, and with no window, a lamp having to be used in the day time. The walls were black with slime, and in spite of being very tired I could get but little rest during the night, my unfortunate body being invaded by hosts of vermin of all sorts. I left this at an early hour the next morning, being only too glad to get away. During my travels I have been forced to take refuge in some curiously dirty places, but this inn will remain fixed in my mind as containing the most varied collection of the most disagreeable things that I have ever met with at one time. We had breakfast on a spur of the mountains looking over the Tung River, whose course we had now again met, and which here takes a direction almost due north. The road leads partly past a precipice from which a headland projects, and here it has to be cut into the face in such a way that the rocks hang over the traveller's head. The path is a little wider than usual, and at this spot a dwarf wall is built on the outer side. This is a precaution for safety rarely seen in the country. A short distance further and a sudden descent takes us into the valley of the Tung, up which we proceed till a sharp turn to the left brings us suddenly into the town of Lu-ting-chiao, which is built on both banks of the Tung River, the two parts ot the town being connected by a suspension bridge—a thing one would hardly expect to see in this remote region. It is, however, a thoroughly good piece of work, having substantial stone piers to carry chains, which are made of iron of a good inch in diameter, the ends of which are secured to the rocks at the back. The footway is about twelve feet wide and is also hung by chains, the boards forming it not being fastened down. This remarkable bridge is about 120 yards long, and is perhaps 150 feet above the highest level of the Tung River. In the street at each end is a bazaar where goods and provisions are sold. I was heartily laughed at by the natives when crossing, for the oscillation was so great as to cause me some alarm, there being no hand rail. I therefore made a halt in the middle, waiting for it to get steady again before proceeding. They being accustomed to it can of course cross without any hesitation.

After getting across I heard that there were some French missionaries at Cha-pa, a short distance down the river, and instead of going on the direct road I decided to visit them, and therefore made a sharp turn to the left. The road was in a place extremely dangerous, being merely a groove cut into an almost precipitous abutment, composed of shale. This foothold—for it is nothing more, and barely that—has to be constantly renewed by anybody who wishes to pass, for in wet weather the shale is washed away, and in dry weather it crumbles. A false step would send a traveller over the slippery surface into the torrent of the Tung River, perhaps a hundred feet beneath, and as, in which, owing to its violence, a boat can hardly live, except in the most quiet places, even the most expert swimmer would have little or no chance of saving his life, if even that had been left to him after the fall. There is considerable traffic past this dangerous place, and it was curious to notice that though such a capital bridge had been constructed such a short distance away, that no effort had been made to improve the road here.

Probably, if a little labour was expended, the solid rock would be reached, and a fairly good and permanent road could then be easily made. We got to Chapa at 4 P.M., and found the missionaries, who gave us a hearty welcome, and were astonished at seeing us. Heavy rain fell just as we arrived, and some time afterwards, as we were sitting in the verandah, talking and smoking, a noise resembling rapidly approaching thunder was heard. On going to the back of the mission-house, where there was a garden, at the end of which was a dry watercourse, we were just in time to see a mass of turbid water, bearing along huge blocks of granite weighing many tons each, break over a precipice, nearly two hundred feet high, with a deafening roar, and plunge into the watercourse beneath. In a moment the flood was passing the bottom of the garden, but the scene of the wildly rushing water is more than my pen is able to describe. A brown-coloured flood dashed furiously along, bearing with it large masses of granite, and tossing them about as if they were mere chips. These were violently thrown against each other and against the bed of the course, with such force as to make the ground tremble beneath our feet.

K

The suddenness of the whole thing—the tremendous noise, the terrible exhibition of the power of a flood of water to toss enormous boulders about like playthings—combined to fix the scene indelibly upon my mind, but no description can do any justice to it.

In about three hours it was all over, and a small stream of water only ran along the course so short a time before in raging flood. It was caused, I have no doubt, by the hot weather we had lately experienced, and the heavy rain acting on the snow on the mountain ranges, perhaps some miles distant.

I slept at the mission-house that night, it being a treat to get clean lodgings after what I had gone through in some of the Chinese inns. The missionaries were very hospitable. They are under their bishop, who resides at Ta-tsien-lu.

On July 3 we left the mission station at 8 A.M., and found a difficulty almost immediately, for the storm of last night had washed part of the road away. I had hired some mules the evening before, but these now could not proceed, and had to be left, we having to travel on foot again as usual. I noticed the wrecks of many houses that had been built on low-lying ground, some having been washed away, others being filled with mud and rendered uninhabitable. These would all be put to rights again in the course of a few weeks, the walls rebuilt or cleared out, as might be necessary; and it is curious to note that though they are probably washed away or damaged every other year or so, they are invariably reconstructed or repaired, the idea of moving to higher and safer ground not apparently entering into the owners' heads. The Tung River to-day was a thick roaring torrent, full of huge boulders and whirlpools. The general direction of the road was now nearly due north. It was very rocky, winding among the spurs of the mountains, and varying from 150 to 1,500 feet above the level of the river, which made it hard work for ourselves and the coolies. There was a great deal of traffic, however, as I noticed tobacco, salt, and tea being taken to Ta-tsien-lu from the lower parts of Sze-chuen, and hides, musk, deer-horns, and medicines going south, all carried by coolies.

Descending into a valley, a tributary of the Tung was crossed by means of a good stone bridge, with the usual coolie rest-house at the end; and ascending, we passed round a high headland, where I noticed large quantities of fossil shells. A few miles further on and Wa-ssu is seen. Prickly pears grow here, this being the first time I saw them. The fruit is used for food. Very fine peaches, apricots, and apples are largely grown, and sent to the market at Ta-tsien-lu. Wa-ssu is a small place, and we stopped the night there. Snow is seen just before the village is reached, high up on the mountains.

On July 4 the road to Ta-tsien-lu led up a very deep gorge, with immense mountains on each side. A remarkably clear stream ran by the side, and here and there fell into deep blue pools. The scenery was magnificent, and the illustration gives but a faint idea of its grandeur. Views up ravines disclosed snow-capped mountains, below which were forests of dark pine, and the different zones of vegetation could be distinctly traced. Just below the snow, grass was growing, and then in rotation followed pine forests, rhododendrons, mixed evergreens, and then in valleys sub-tropical plants. I should here note that the vegetation is more Tibetan in character than Chinese. On the road I noticed a single rope suspension bridge over a river. This consisted of a bamboo cable about three inches in diameter, stretched across about 120 feet above the water, and having a free running plaited bamboo ring upon it. From this ring an inverted T-piece, with the shank about four feet long, hung, and light hauling lines were attached to it and to each bank. The traveller seats himself on the cross of the T, and then, the cable of course being in a curve, on letting go from the bank his own weight carries him half-way, or

WA-SSU-KOU GORGE.

more, across. He now takes the hauling line, and pulls himself up the curve to the other bank.

The city of Ta-tsien-lu is not seen by the traveller until he is close to the gates, and on entering, the streets are found to be crowded with a strange mixture of races. The houses are certainly Chinese, but the population is a mixture of all the nations of Asia, Tibetans predominating. I made my way through the city, and, passing out by the south gate, soon found the house of the Roman Catholic Bishop—Monseigneur Biet—who received me very kindly, and interested himself in getting rooms at an inn in the city, the same place that Captain Gill and Mr. Baber had stopped at.

CHAPTER X

TA-TSIEN-LU

Meet Mr. Rockhill—His journey—Missionaries give great assistance—Christian collectors—Hard life and devotion of the missionaries—Description of the inn—Prayer papers—Caravans—Caravan drivers—Their dress—The landlady's wealth—Value of gold—City of Ta-tsien-lu—Its inhabitants—Their dress and arms—Lamas—Funeral rites of a lama—Brick tea—Loads carried by coolies—Trade—Distance travelled by caravans—Currency—Sealing-wax—Women's feast—Sanscrit inscriptions—Despatch carriers between Pekin and Lhassa—Departure of Mr. Rockhill—Misfortunes of his men—Tibetan dogs—Expedition to Chet-tu—Poor lodgings—*Crossoptilon Tibetanum* seen—*Parnassius Imperator*—Expedition to the north—Shooting *Crossoptilon*—Preparations for departure.

On my arrival at the inn I found Mr. Rockhill, an American, who had been previously attached to their legation at Pekin, and who had travelled from that place through the practically unknown region on the boundary between China and Tibet. I had been told by Monseigneur Biet that he was there, and was agreeably surprised that I should have an English-speaking fellow traveller living in the same house with me for at least some days.

I do not know how to sufficiently thank Bishop Biet and the Fathers Soulié, Mossot and Dejean for all their kindness and attention to me during my stay.

TA-TSIEN-LU, FROM THE SOUTH.

Everything in their power was done, and as they spoke both Tibetan and Chinese, and were well acquainted with the peculiar ways and manners of the natives, it may be easily understood that their assistance was invaluable. Bishop Biet, a man with a highly cultivated mind and refined taste, has been here, or rather in the district, for twenty-five years, and here he will in all probability end his days, for he told me that the missionary bishops are rarely, if ever, recalled by the Pope. The last European he saw before Mr. Rockhill, who, by the way, is an American, and myself, was Mr. Baber in 1879, and this is 1889. His brother, also a missionary, was murdered in Manchuria, and here both he and the Fathers have to be extremely cautious even now, for the lamas bear them no goodwill. My collectors were all Christians, brought up from childhood by the Bishop and the Fathers, and were in a much more civilised state than the Buddhist Tibetans and mixed Chinese, who refused to work for me. All the Roman Catholic missionaries had a very hard life, and I think that people at home have very little idea of the sacrifices they make for the sake of their religion. Beyond having cleaner, and perhaps, in a trifling way, better houses than the natives, there is no difference in their mode of life. They seldom see civilised people, and yet have done much to civilise the almost savage races among whom they dwell. Their food is coarse and often scanty, and their lives are frequently in danger. The Bishop himself now seldom leaves his house, but does all the Church work there through the Fathers and the considerable number of converts that have been made.

The winter weather is now too severe for him, and in the autumn he goes down to Cha-pa, just below Lu-ting-chiao, and remains there till the spring. He was not in good health when I last saw him.

On July 8 I took his photograph, and he was delighted at the idea of sending copies to his friends and relations. My camera was undoubtedly the first that had ever been in this region, and by its agency the Bishop was enabled to send to his friends of twenty-five years ago a tolerably faithful picture of himself. The devotion of the French missionaries in general to the cause of their religion deserves notice. No work is too hard for them, no living too poor. They are not deterred by epidemics of sickness or by threatened massacre. They have simply devoted their lives to the propagation of their religion, and nothing can turn them from their purpose. Much they have done, but much more remains to be done; and it struck me forcibly, during my travels, that they, above all others, are the most determined that it *shall* be done.

The inn in which I had my quarters was fairly comfortable. In front was a yard and stabling for a few horses, and a pole was erected in it from which strings of paper prayers hung fluttering in the wind. Round the walls also bits of stick were inserted here and there and similarly ornamented. The roof of the kitchen was flat, and on it there was a small dome-shaped erection of clay, in which every day, at about five o'clock in the afternoon, the branches of a sort of coniferous plant were burnt with religious ceremony.

Caravans used to stop here, and on their arrival the beasts of burden were unloaded in the yard and then driven along a passage running through the house to an enclosure at the back, where they were left for the night. The animals used were horses, or a cross-breed between the yak and a cow, a much smaller animal than the wild yak. The drivers are all Tibetan, and are a rough muscular set of men wearing their hair hanging over their faces, their skins being tanned a dark brown colour. They wear a loose brown woollen coat reaching to the knees, and fastened round the waist with a belt, through which the upper part is pulled up till it falls over and hides the girdle, forming a substitute for pockets. Raw hide boots reaching to just below the knee are worn, and a curiously shaped cowl for the head with a flap hanging down behind, in the middle of which is a circular red patch, completes their costume. They also wear, but whether as an ornament or not I could not find out, a long thick pigtail, plaited up out of coarse black hair and ornamented with silver bands, in some of which turquoises or pieces of red coral are set.

The landlady of the inn was a Tibetan, whose husband was at Lhassa, and who was, I believe, an interpreter. She was very comfortably off as far as I could judge, and one day she showed me a great part of her wealth, which consisted of massive gold ornaments of rough manufacture. It is a common practice among the women here to have their fortunes in jewellery, because, I imagine, there are no banks or safe places where money can be kept. Gold, I may here mention, has not the same relative value to silver as it has in Lower China, but is considerably cheaper.

The city of Ta-tsien-lu is most irregularly built, the houses being of all shapes and sizes, the roadways merely layers of large stones, and a stream runs through its centre from south to north.

It is inhabited principally by Chinese and Tibetans, the former being generally the merchants and shopkeepers, the latter for the most part employed in the caravan trade. All Tibetans are dressed in much the same way as I have before described, those not being employed in caravans wearing a felt hat, if a hat is worn at all, instead of a cowl. Certain of the more wealthy wear

STREET LEADING TO SOUTH GATE, TA-TSIEN-LU.

on occasions a grey felt hat, perhaps a foot high. No Tibetan is ever without a wooden bowl, sometimes lined with silver, from which he eats his porridge or drinks his tea. He also invariably carries a small neat tinder-box, usually with the steel attached to it, the flint being carried inside. These two articles when not in use are carried in the folds of his long coarse coat.

All races of Asiatics may be seen in the streets, many being tall, fine, fierce-looking specimens of humanity, armed with long guns, daggers and swords. Their fire-arms are as a rule of no great use, being of the obsolete type so frequently seen among such people, but the owners value them highly; and though I wished to bring some home as curiosities, the price asked was so high as to prevent my purchasing. Many lamas are seen at all times in the town, there being a large lamasery just outside. They may be told by their scarlet cloaks and shaven heads, and their music while at prayers is heard all day long. Monseigneur Biet informed me that, while he was at Batang, a lama of high rank died. The body was carried to a lofty plateau, the flesh was then cut off the bones, and the bones crushed and mixed with flour. Both were then given to the vultures, and the whole body was thus satisfactorily disposed of. Tibetan women work hard. They collect firewood on the mountain slopes, and do much out-of-door work which the Chinese women are unable to do.

A large quantity of tea comes into Ta-tsien-lu, principally from Ya-chow-fu. It is of a very coarse description, and is made up in slabs about forty inches long, nine wide, and three and a half thick, weighing perhaps twelve to fifteen pounds each, and are wrapped in matting. They are carried by coolies, who travel by way of the Lu-ting bridge, this being the only place where the Tung River can be crossed in the district. The loads carried by the coolies are enormous, and run from 200 lbs. to considerably over 300 lbs., the slabs of tea being packed on a light wooden frame, and reaching high above the coolie's head, the frame having two rope loops at the upper end, through which the arms are passed. A T stick is always carried, and when resting, the weight of the burden is taken by the top of the stick, the bottom being on the ground. Bishop Biet showed me an iron safe about two feet high that had been carried from Ya-chow by one man. At Ta-tsien-lu the slabs of tea are cut up into so-called bricks, which are then packed in hide and taken by the caravans to all parts of Tibet. Tobacco and salt are also taken by the caravans, having been first imported from China, and they bring from Tibet for export to the East, hides, deer-horns, musk and medicinal plants.

Some of the caravans travel enormous distances, one going regularly to Tishulumbo, to the westward of Lhassa, and about 1,500 miles from Ta-tsien-lu. They are six months on the road. Indian rupees are here plentiful, and are a recognised currency. Russian roubles are also found, and in increasing numbers.

I found a very useful kind of sealing-wax here. It is made from the refuse of a Tibetan dye, and does not melt or bend from the heat of the weather. It is very light, and of a dark brown colour.

One day there was a women's feast at the inn; what the occasion was I do not know, but about twenty met, Chinese and Tibetan, all dressed in their best, the former in silks and satins, with hair well oiled and cheeks painted and powdered, the latter in dark woollen blouse and trousers, with boots up to the knee. They all wore as much jewellery as possible, of gold and silver, the latter having turquoises and coral set in it, and being roughly enamelled. The earrings worn were very large, with chains hanging down, and the remainder of the ornaments took the form of long chains, bracelets, and brooches, all being of rough manufacture. They met at about two o'clock in the afternoon, and appeared to enjoy themselves very much till six, when they dispersed.

In the roads, in various places near the town, large

heaps of broken stone slabs may be seen, covered with inscriptions in Sanscrit character. They are not understood by the natives, but are held in great respect, and if a piece gets broken off or thrown into the road, it is always carefully replaced. The Chinese take no notice of these heaps.

This town is on the high road between Pekin and Lhassa, and sometimes the Government messenger may be seen passing through. The system is curious, and it seems to be indispensable that a despatch of any importance *must* be carried the whole distance by one man. The best horses are procured for him to ride upon, and he never stops except to change horses, to the saddle of which he is tied. He is accompanied by two soldiers, who are changed at every station, on the arrival at which a fresh horse is always found ready, and fresh guards in attendance. The courier is untied from the horse, given a raw egg to eat, mounted and tied to a fresh horse, and proceeds on his journey. I was informed that this excessively hard work proves fatal to many couriers.

On July 11 Mr. Rockhill left on his return journey, which he made to Shanghai by, I believe, the same road that I had come up, viz. by land to Kia-ting-fu, and then down the river by native boat to Ichang, where he would be able to finish his journey by steamer.

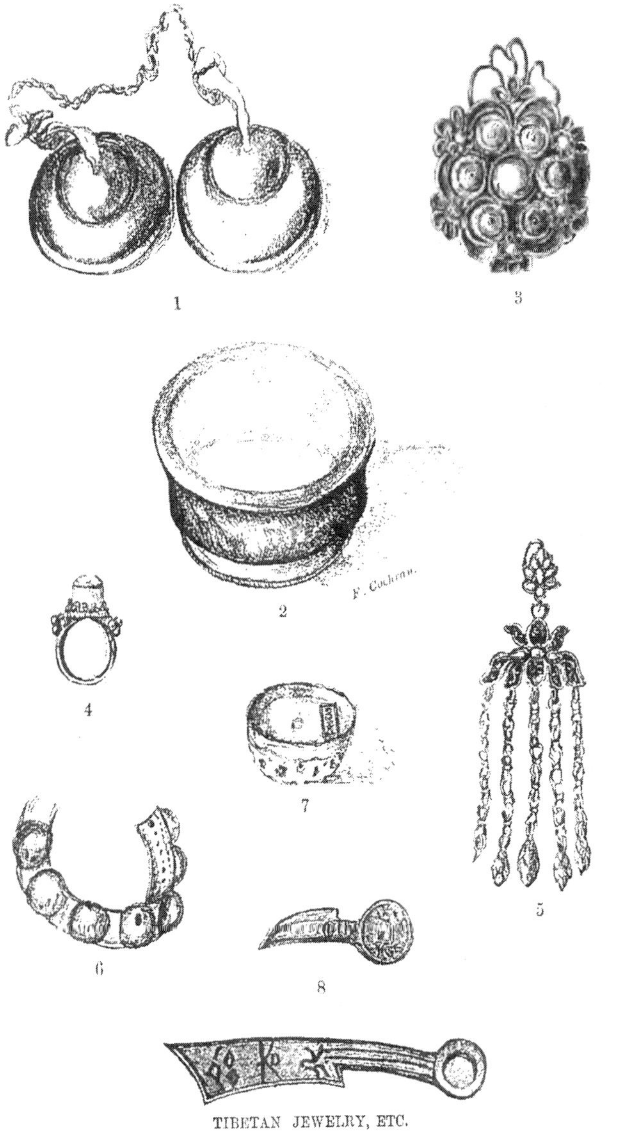

TIBETAN JEWELRY, ETC.

1. Bells carried by lamas. 2. Tibetan tsamba bowl, made of wood and lined with silver.
3. Tibetan brooch: silver, turquoise, and coral. 4. Tibetan ring: silver, with a turquoise.
5. Tibetan ear-ring: silver, and turquoises.
6. Part of Tibetan woman's belt: leather, with polished pebbles stitched on; length about 9 feet, weight 3½ lbs.
7. Chinese shoe silver. 8. Very old sword cash from Sui-fu.

He was much put out before leaving because some of his men had not come in, though he had been nearly three weeks, I think, waiting for them. Among the things that they were bringing were two Tibetan dogs, one of which he made a present to me, if they should ever arrive. Seven days after he left the men came in with a long tale of misfortunes to relate. The lamas, they said, had treated them very badly. They refused to supply them with fodder for their horses, and consequently they had lost some from starvation. They were then bound hand and foot for ten days, while the lamas sent to Cheng-tu for orders about them. When their messenger returned he brought directions for their liberation. All this trouble was caused by their travelling without passports. They brought the dogs safely, however, and I much regret that I was unable to bring either home, the female dying at Hankow and the male in the Mediterranean. The latter was an enormous beast, the largest dog I have ever seen, with a black shaggy coat and tan-coloured legs. He had a broad muzzle, and was very powerful and fierce. This breed is peculiar to a province or district called Deggi, and even the local king at Ta-tsien-lu has to send there for them if he wants them pure. The female was smaller, with a smooth coat, but of the same colour, black and tan. She was a Sifan dog, and not so savage as the male, but sly and treacherous. These dogs are used by all the caravan drivers to protect their merchandise at night. When they arrive at a camping-place the beasts of burden have their loads removed and stacked together. They are then covered with a tent of some sort, and the dogs are secured to stakes all round. If they caught a thief they would pull him down in a moment, and probably kill him.

On July 25 I left Ta-tsien-lu for a few days, travelling to Chet-tu, a Tibetan village about ten miles to the westward. The mountains here rise to an elevation of 15,000 feet, and I found lodging in a stone-built hut in the valley beneath. There were two rooms in the hut, one being inhabited by the owners, the other by the cows, pigs, cats, dogs, and fowls belonging to them—and ourselves. It was not possible to get much rest, and the place was very dirty. The roof let the rain in, and the wind whistled through crevices in the walls. Everything, however, was not bad, for I found I could get excellent milk. In the morning I ascended the mountain to see if I could find any *Crossoptilon Tibetanum*. After a hard walk I saw a fine cock within ten yards, and my cartridge missed fire. This was the first one I had ever seen wild, and the only one I saw during the day. It was a most annoying thing. I was not far now from the snow, and I found many flowers growing, principally annuals, and of several species. This district is rich in *Thecla*, and I have taken as many as 300 *T. Bieti* in one morning with my forceps off the droppings of the baggage animals on the Lhassa road.

On the 29th I returned to Ta-tsien-lu, having made a good collection. I had now a good series of *Parnassius Imperator* and of many other species, the best hours for collecting being between eight and eleven in the forenoon, for afterwards a strong breeze sprung up usually, and lasted till nearly five.

On August 10 I made a trip to the northward, and as there were no villages in the mountains I intended to visit I took a Tibetan tent with me. These are made of Chinese cloth embroidered with blue, and are used by the Tibetans in the summer, when they make trips to the mineral springs in the mountains, in which they bathe. At 5 P.M. I had arrived at an altitude of 11,000 feet. The tent was pitched and all made snug. The scenery was magnificent, the snow above us commencing at an altitude of about 16,000 feet, the country between being well wooded, principally with pines. The next day I shot a few *Crossoptilon Tibetanum* in the morning, but none in the afternoon. The country is very difficult to get over at all, the slopes being very steep, and in other places large quantities of stones and boulders may be found, piled together probably by avalanches, and in such a loose way that anybody walking over them might chance to set one moving, and that would most likely set a large number rolling down in a most dangerous way. I saw at least a hundred of the *Crossoptilon*, many in places where it was impossible to shoot.

Père Soulié came up and stayed a day and a night, and on the 14th we returned to Ta-tsien-lu, and I at once made preparations for departure. My journey there was not originally contemplated, but I saw such an interesting country before me that I resolved, if possible, to return the following year. I had, however, considerable collections at Ta-tien-chih, and these, with what I had collected at Ta-tsien-lu, I was anxious to get together and send home as early as possible. In addition to what I had when I left the former place, I expected to have a large quantity gathered by the collectors I had left behind.

CAMP NORTH OF TA-TSIEN-LU. TIBETAN TENT.

CHAPTER XI

RETURN JOURNEY TO ICHANG

Departure for Wa-ssu—Difficulty at Fu-lin—Huang-mu-chang—Road lost—So-i-ling Pass at night—Arrive at Ta-tien-chih at midnight—Collectors work—Horses procured—Guard of soldiers—Arrive at Kia-ting-fu—Carelessness with mails—Go to my boat—Very heavy flood—Great loss of life—False rumours concerning the object of my journey—Inspection of boat by Tao-tai—Visit to city—Lowban procures flag—Leave for Ichang—Destruction of village—Boat aground in wrong channel—Pass Sui-fu—Lu-chau—Delayed by heavy rain—Arrival at Chung-king—Delayed by high river at Quei-chow-fu—Wrecks of junks—Pass the Sin-tan and Ta-tung Rapids.—Waterfalls.

On August 15 I finished my packing; and after having thanked Bishop Biet and the Fathers for their extreme kindness and invaluable assistance, telling my collectors at the same time that I hoped to be able to engage them the following summer, I left for Wa-ssu at 2 P.M. and arrived at 7.30.

My return journey was taken by the same road that I had come by, and I crossed the Fei-yueh-ling Pass on August 18, arriving at Fu-lin on the 20th. Here, again, I had difficulties, for they were most inhospitable to me on my first passing through the town. Now I found the greatest difficulty in getting a room to sleep in, but at last I managed to get a den in which to pass the night. It had no ventilation; the stench was abominable and the heat almost unbearable; but it was better than nothing.

My coolies went off to smoke opium as usual. It is a most pernicious habit, no doubt, but they will do it whenever they have money, and it has become with most of them such a habit that they cannot do without it.

I was glad to leave the heat and discomfort of Fu-lin as soon as I could the next morning, and after a hard day's work over bad roads I got to Chin-ki-za, in a delightful climate 6,000 feet above the sea level, at 6 P.M., and on the 22nd I reached Huang-mu-chang, where I found Père Martin, who gave me a warm welcome.

On August 23rd I sent my coolies on in the morning to Ta-tien-chih, keeping two only with me, my object in staying behind being to take a photograph of Père Martin, who was very anxious to have it done. Having accomplished this, satisfactorily as I thought, I made a start at 2 P.M., but had a most unfortunate journey. The coolie whom I had trusted as a guide missed the way, and for some time did not find out what a mistake he had made. In the end we were about ten miles on a wrong road and had to return. We reached the top of the So-i-ling Pass, 8,770 feet, just as it became pitch dark, and the descent was absolutely dangerous.

Luckily we were able to make torches of dry bamboo, but even then the road was rather alarming. To finish, we arrived at Ta-tien-chih at midnight, fearfully hungry and worn out, but could obtain nothing to eat except rice.

The following day I sent to recall all the collectors I had left behind, and upon looking over their work, both entomological and botanical, I found that they had done very well, and I had much reason to be pleased with their exertions. I was very busy packing up all day, getting the things dried as well as possible, engaging coolies and horses, of which I was fortunate enough to procure three, one being for Mr. Kricheldorff, one for the cook, and the third for myself.

On August 26 I started with twenty-four coolies and found the horse a great assistance. I was unable to ride all day, the road being, in many places, too dangerous. Chin-kou-ho was reached in the evening, and here I found three Yamen runners waiting for me, they having been sent by the local mandarin, whom I had informed, at his special desire, of my return to Wa-shan. This part of the road, that is to say between Wa-shan and Kia-ting-fu, is always considered to be dangerous from its proximity to the Lolo frontier; and I believe attacks are more frequently made here than in the districts further west and north.

On the 30th Su-chi was reached, and from here I finished the journey with my men in two sampans, arriving at Kia-ting-fu at 4 P.M. The missionaries, Messrs. Ririe and Vale, came to see me, and I was much disappointed when they informed me that there were no letters.

I then made inquiries of the Chinese agent, as he had instructions to detain any letters for me, but he also told me that there were none. Later on, when I arrived at Chung-king, I saw Messrs. Butterfield and Swires' agent (also a Chinese), and he told me that a large parcel had been sent to Kia-ting-fu to the care of the agent there. Subsequently I discovered that by a piece of carelessness they had been returned to Chung-king, the consequence being that I never received them until some time after my return to Ichang, the postage charged being very nearly ten shillings.

On my arrival I took up my quarters at once in the boat, which I was glad to find safe. The lowban had had an anxious time, he told me, on account of the flood which occurred in July; and in this he was borne out by the statements of the missionaries and the Chinese themselves, who declared that nothing like it had occurred for a hundred years. In one night the river rose fifty feet, flowing into the city through the gates, destroying houses and property of all kinds.

During the night the cries of the unfortunate people whose houses were flooded could be heard imploring assistance, but none could be rendered. Hundreds of boats and sampans were dashed to atoms in the roaring flood of the river, and the loss of life was appalling. Large junks broke adrift, and some were not got under control until they had been drifted 800 li down the river.

During my absence I found that the most extraordinary stories had circulated among the natives as to the object of my journey. Some said that I was kidnapping children and making medicine out of their eyes for my photographic apparatus. It was impossible, they said, for anybody to take such pictures without. Other reports said that I was catching and killing snakes so large that it required five men to carry them. Then, again, the old story was revived, that I had an infernal machine in the boat, and was only waiting for a favourable opportunity to utterly destroy the city. All these things had been reported to the Tao-tai, but of course he knew far better than to pay any attention to them; still, the rumours were so persistent that he felt bound, as a matter of form, to personally inspect the boat again, after having done which he did all in his power to reassure the people that no evil thing was in the boat, and that no danger was to be apprehended.

There being no students in the town now, I was able to visit it, and found a fine city with good shops and the people civil. There is a large trade done in silk, and the town is famous for its embroidery. There is also a considerable trade in the white vegetable wax.

I was now busy packing, drying, and stowing away the collections in the boat. This place is very unhealthy at this time of year, and the weather was very rainy, but advantage was taken of every gleam of sunshine to spread things out on the roof of the cabin to dry, damp being one's principal enemy in this district.

The river was now high, and the navigation dangerous. I therefore engaged a pilot who was said to have a good local knowledge.

All being at last arranged and ready to start, the lowban came on board with two Yamen runners, who were to accompany me down the river. He informed me that if we had not got a flag we should be forced to stop at all the hsiens, or smaller towns, and that he could procure such a flag. He also said that it would save us from much annoyance from the natives, who were badly disposed towards foreigners. I told him that I only intended to stop at the fus, or large cities, and gave him an hour to procure the flag. He then went on shore, and after a while returned with it. It was of white calico, about a yard wide by three long, and had some characters painted in black on it. I have not entered into a full description of the procuring of this flag, as I shall have more to say about it later on. The boat was under way at 8 A.M. on September 4, and the journey down, with the river high, was made at a very different rate of speed from the journey up. The first day 280 li were made, and the boat secured only eighty-five li from Sui-fu. A place was passed where, on the voyage up, a thriving village was situated. Not a trace of it now remained, it having been utterly destroyed by the flood and many of its inhabitants drowned.

During the day the pilot took a wrong channel and ran the boat on a bank. She swung round and stuck fast. The rudder had to be unshipped, and some of the crew getting overboard gradually worked her off into deep water. I had purchased a sampan as a measure of precaution at Kia-ting-fu, so that in case of my boat getting on a rock the collections might be landed. She, however, on this occasion took the proper channel, and was swept past us in a moment, and I need hardly add that it was impossible for her to return against the current to our assistance. She would only be of any service by keeping at a considerable distance astern.

On arriving at Sui-fu the next day I got rid of the pilot and got another. I stayed here only long enough for this and to send a letter that I had brought from Bishop Biet at Ta-tsien-lu to the Bishop. The distance made was 365 li. On September 6 I passed Lu-chau, where a considerable trade seems to be going on, especially in timber. A head wind stopped us a little and several dangerous places were passed. This pilot seems to be up to his work. The huloes are kept going to give the boat way through the water, just sufficient to make her answer her helm. A village was passed to-day where a robbery took place on our journey up, and part of the crew landed in the sampan to try and recover some of the stolen articles. Directly the object of their visit was understood the natives turned out in force, and they had to beat a hasty retreat, not without having received many hard blows from stools, bamboos, or anything that first came to hand. Made 305 li to-day and anchored, being now 290 li from Chung-king.

September 7.—Could not start to-day till 7, and then soon had to anchor again, the rain being so heavy that it was impossible to see far enough ahead. This was very annoying, as I had quite expected to reach Chung-king, but, as it was, had to anchor eighty li from it. However, I got there on the 8th, and stayed till the 10th, during which time I paid visits to the Bishop and the Fathers at the French Mission. They were very glad to hear about Bishop Biet. Mr. Cockburn, the British Resident, very kindly asked me to stay at his house, and I gladly accepted his hospitality. He lives on high ground at some distance from the river, in a good Chinese house, which he has made very comfortable. It is situated in the middle of the city, but has a fine open compound where there is plenty of fresh air; a matter of considerable importance where the climate generally is close and damp. It is, however, not a convenient place for taking exercise from, as if the road is taken inland nearly half the day is spent in getting out of the town and its suburbs, the same objection holding good if the river is crossed. I was informed that in 1880 no less than 150,000,000 lb. of cotton passed the town, having come up from Hankow for sale in Western China. There is a large archery ground in the western part of the city situated on high land, and from which a splendid view of the city is obtained. I much regretted that when I was there I had not taken my camera, for though the weather was dull I should have much liked to have had two or three negatives. After having said good-bye to all my friends, among whom I should mention Mr. and Mrs. Wilson, missionaries, I left on September 10, finding the travelling on the river very bad and dangerous. Fourteen men were required to keep the boat under any sort of control, and the bow sweep was in frequent use. On the following day the river was, if possible, worse; but the rate of speed was high, about 300 li being made each day. On September 12 the boat was made fast off the village of Hu-lin, and the people were very disagreeable. My dogs were chained up on the beach, and they came down and stoned them. Fearing that someone might get bitten, I was obliged to move the dogs into the boat.

On the 13th I arrived at Quei-chow-fu, having travelled 420 li during the day, and here I was delayed till the 16th, the river being dangerously high. I found several hundreds of junks waiting here till the river should fall sufficiently to make the passage safe, and I heard that a day or two ago three junks were knocked to pieces at a bad place a short distance below. Their crews were all drowned, and one of them had a hundred souls on board. Sometimes the navigation is stopped here for weeks at a time. There are certain marks on the city walls, and when the water is above the highest it is not considered safe to descend the river; also when it is below the lowest it is dangerous.

On the 16th the water had fallen a little, and it was considered safe to travel. A run of 420 li was made during the day, and on the 17th, which I thought the most exciting day of all, the Me-tan and Lu-kan Gorges were passed, and the Sin-tan and Ta-tung Rapids, the boat being secured in a backwater about thirty li below the latter. This was a difficult place to get into, for if the boat was not huloed into it at exactly the right moment she was liable to be swept past, and then it could not be regained against the stream. All the way down the boat appeared to be a mere toy in the stream. The utmost skill is necessary just to keep the way on, so that she could be steered. Sometimes she was swept into a whirlpool, and could not be got out for half an hour or so, just being drifted round and round. In the wider and shallower parts the shingle can be distinctly heard rolling along the river bed under the boat.

Many small waterfalls were seen during the last part of the voyage down the river, some being of great height and all very picturesque. They had been caused by the exceptionally heavy rain of the last few days flooding the watercourses.

CHAPTER XII

SECOND JOURNEY TO TA-TSIEN-LU

Arrival at Ichang—Story of the lowban's flag—Despatch collections—Leopard on the river bank—Trip to Hankow—Telegraph line—Official letters concerning my boat—Prepare for journey up river—Boat damaged on rock—Curious pagoda at Shi-po-chia—Arrive at Chung-king—Collector sent to Quei-chau—Sui-fu—Kia-ting-fu—Prepare for journey—Despatch coolies to Kia-kiang—Omêi-hsien—Wan-nien-tze—Bronze elephant and Buddha—Peculiar tea—Tibetan worshipper—The summit of Mount Omêi—Bronze temple—Pagoda—Tremendous precipice—Tigers on the mountain—Suicides—View of the Snowy Mountains—Number of temples and priests on the mountain—Kia-kiang—Arrival at Ya-chow—Bamboo rafts on Ya River—Yung-ching-hsien — Tai-hsiang-ling-kwan Pass—Ching-chi-hsien—Bad road—Arrival at Ta-tsien-lu.

On September 19 I arrived at Ichang at 3 P.M. It had been raining heavily all day, and the river was rising. My boat was anchored opposite the British Consulate. The next morning the British Consul came on board and asked me what flag I had been flying, as a deputation of leading citizens had waited upon him that morning saying that his Minister had arrived, and that they were anxious to pay their respects. I showed it to him: this was the flag that I allowed the lowban to procure at Kia-ting-fu, and he read immediately that it bore the characters of the late Sir Harry Parkes. Upon calling upon the lowban for an explanation he smiled and informed me that it was a 'No. 1 piecee flag,' and for him no doubt it was so, for he had made use of its protection to smuggle a quantity of various kinds of excisable articles, such as salt, musk, and medicines, past the lekin stations, the Customs authorities not interfering with a Minister's boat. I had noticed at Kia-ting-fu that the crew were busy shipping a lot of salt—so much, in fact, that I had to put a stop to it, as we were getting too deep in the water—but that it was all to be smuggled under a false flag never dawned upon me. I certainly noticed with some pride that at places the boat attracted a good deal of attention, the people firing crackers, &c.; but I put it down to her smart appearance or to the presence of a mandarin whose boat I had not observed.

I was now very busy drying, packing, and sending off the collections I had got together, and after all were despatched I spent the time in shooting at different places on the banks of the river that I visited in my boat. There is very fair sport to be obtained, wildfowl being plentiful, but difficult to approach. Pheasants abound in places where there is sufficient cover, and a few deer are to be found. The weather generally was fine but cold, and the river in the winter had run down to its lowest level.

On November 15 a leopard suddenly appeared on

the bank of the river, right in the middle of a crowded boating population. An old man foolishly attacked it with an axe, upon which it sprang on him and severely lacerated his head, neck, and shoulders with its claws and teeth, but was quickly despatched before doing any further damage. The old man died from the effects of his wounds a few days after. Such a thing had never been heard of before.

I had just finished breakfast at the time, and, seeing a crowd, walked down to see what the matter was, accompanied by one of the Customs staff. On seeing me someone in the crowd declared that the beast had escaped from my boat, whereupon I was roundly abused by the wife of the wounded man, and in less time than it takes to write this I was accused of having brought down in my boat elephants, lions, tigers, and all sorts of impossible animals. The mob quickly got so threatening that we thought it advisable to retire with as much speed as was consistent with dignity.

In December I left in my boat for Hankow, more for a change than anything else, for neither Mr. Kricheldorff nor myself had fully recovered from the hardships of our journey to Ta-tsien-lu, and I thought that the journey would do us both good. We went down leisurely, and arrived at Hankow on the 29th. Here I remained till February 4, and having previously sent my boat back to Ichang, I went up with Mr. Kricheldorff in the steamer *Kiang-tung*. During my stay at Hankow, being rather undecided as to whether I should proceed again to Ta-tsien-lu, I sent some collectors, both entomological and botanical, there overland; but having decided before leaving to go there myself in the boat, I was able to stop them by telegraph at Ichang. The telegraph line is laid from Hankow to Ichang, then, still following the river, to Chung-king, from which place it goes direct to Cheng-tu. The local mandarins are responsible for the safety of the line, and repairs are done by workmen who are stationed at intervals. Messages are sent in English, Chinese not being, I believe, adapted to the purpose.

When describing my boat in a former chapter, I mentioned that I had the cabin and topsides painted white with the object of keeping the cabin as cool as possible. The native boats and junks are varnished all over with the vegetable varnish, and present a light-brown colour. My boat was therefore a very conspicuous object, and, being so uncommon, very likely to attract attention. This I found she did, and I think that her colour was the principal cause of the attack made at Kia-ting-fu; and, as mentioned before, she was scraped and varnished while waiting there. During my stay here, however, the following letter and enclosure, which was sent to the Consul, showed that she had attracted attention in a quarter where I had not suspected it.

'*From "Fang" Tao-tai (of Chung-king).*

'Sir,—On the 1st I had the honour to receive from H.E. the Viceroy "Ya" a despatch instructing me forthwith to carry out the request contained in the enclosed communication.

'I have accordingly given the requisite orders to the deputies of this office, and beg to acquaint you with the communication referred to.

'I have &c.'

The Viceroy 'Ya' mentioned in the above is the Viceroy of Sze-chuen, and the enclosure is as under:

'Sir,—Wang-tsun-wen, Prefect of Chung-king, has forwarded a representation from Chow Chow Chao Ch'ng, magistrate of Pa Hshien, that on April 21 last the Chiang-pu sub-prefect sent on under escort the Englishman Pratt and the German trader Kricheldorff, who had come to Chung-king prefecture in their small foreign boat with a Chinese crew, and that on the 24th they proceeded on their journey to Kia-ting-fu, saying in reply to questions that they were purchasing goods as they went along. The Prefect submits that for

Englishmen to enter Sze-chuen in a foreign boat while the question of steam navigation is still under discussion is a most rash proceeding. If at the present time, when people and converts are mutually suspicious, the people of Sze-chuen should assemble and stop them, and trouble should arise, the local authorities would hardly accept the blame of failing to afford efficient protection.

'He had therefore reported for our instructions, and we have replied, we would write for requisite orders to be given. With regard to the question of steam navigation to Chung-king, no decision has yet been come to, although officers have been sent to Ichang to confer with the Consul. The Sze-chuenese are now suspicious and distrustful, and popular feeling is greatly excited. Should they at the sight of a foreign boat collect in a mob and interfere with it, grave trouble would surely follow, for which the local authorities could not be held to blame. We have the honour to request, therefore, that it be stated in the passports of all foreigners who shall hereafter enter Sze-chuen that they must travel by land or hire native boats, and may not any more bring trouble on themselves by attempting to use foreign boats. This is of the last importance, and we have written to Tsung-li Yamen to notify to H. B. Majesty's Minister to transmit the requisite instructions. We beg also that you will instruct the officers at places where passports are issued to act in compliance with our request.

'(Signed) YA, Viceroy of Sze-chuen.'

The boat was evidently taken for one of foreign build because of her colour, and as to the statements said to have been made by Mr. Kricheldorff and myself that we were purchasing goods as we went along, they were mere fabrications.

However, the Consul wrote to Sir John Walsham at Pekin, enclosing a copy of the letter, and I also wrote explaining matters. After I had left on a second journey to Kia-ting-fu a reply came, saying that H. B. Majesty's Minister considered that it was a rash proceeding to have gone as far as Chung-king in a boat that might be mistaken for a foreign one.

I should add that when the boat was varnished all over she attracted no attention whatever.

Arriving at Ichang on February 8, 1890, I set to work at once preparing for the journey up river again, engaging trackers and crew, and seeing that a large supply of boxes, nets, &c., were got on board, and I left for my second trip up the river on February 18, being determined to get to Ta-tsien-lu in time for the earliest species.

At Huang-yang-mu, just beyond the Ichang Gorge,

I saw snow still lying on the sides of the steep hills at the back of the town. The river was now at its lowest, and when in that state the Ta-tung Rapid is not dangerous.

After leaving Quei-chow-fu I was suspicious of two of the men of my crew, my boat having been, I thought, maliciously put upon a rock. One of them was the pilot, and I noticed that he frequently had disagreements with the lowban. I got rid of both of them at an early opportunity. The boat, however, was damaged, and next morning the water was above the cabin floor. She was soon baled out, the leak discovered and temporarily stopped, permanent repairs being made at Yeng-yang-hsien. No serious damage was done, but the delay was annoying.

At Shi-po-chia there is a very curious pagoda, which, instead of being built as usual on the top of a hill, is constructed against an enormous isolated limestone rock about 400 yards from the river bank, where it forms a very conspicuous object, the top of the pagoda appearing just above the rock.

Chung-king was reached on March 12, and I waited till the 17th, Mr. Cockburn very kindly inviting me to stay with him. Here I had to change my trackers and get an up-river crew. I also sent a collector from here to Quei-chau, a poor but interesting province about which very little is known. I had to leave the choice of locality to him, and before leaving I was able, through the kindness of the Resident, to have a paper declaration pasted on his collecting boxes to the effect that they contained no contraband articles. This saved a deal of examination and trouble in passing from Sze-chuen into Quei-chau.

On the 17th I left, accompanied by Mr. Cockburn, who remained with me till the 19th and then returned to Chung-king.

March 29, 1890.—Arrived at Sui-fu, and started up the Min River the next day. This river is very clear, and forms a striking contrast to the muddy Yang-tze. The current, however, is strong, and many extra trackers had to be engaged. On April 3, heavy rain fell and a freshet came down. This made the work still more trying for the trackers, and on the day after the tow rope carried away three times, I am thankful to say without causing any disaster.

April 7.—Arrived at Kia-ting-fu, having been passing through rapids nearly all the way from Sui-fu.

I now sent back the trackers, discharged those of the crew that were not collectors, and left instructions with the latter to work all likely places. As they were now pretty well up in their work, the districts were left to their own judgment. My boat was left in charge of the lowban, as on the former visit; and as she was now varnished brown like all the native craft, instead of being painted white, she attracted little or no attention and there was no trouble given by the authorities.

On April 10, having everything prepared for a stay at Ta-tsien-lu, my boxes, &c., making loads for thirty-five coolies, I sent them off with orders to wait for me at Kia-kiang, as I intended to visit Mount Omêi, it being but little out of the way. I left Kia-ting-fu on the same day, and slept that night at Omêi-hsien. This place supplies all the priests living on Mount Omêi with food, &c., and during the winter large supplies have to be laid in by them, as the road up the mountain is blocked with snow and ice. I noticed skins of a species of armadillo exposed for sale in the shops here.

The next day I proceeded to Wan-nien-tze, situated on the mountain at an elevation of 3,500 feet, the road consisting largely of series of stairs, and many temples were passed. The name signifies 'the temple of 10,000 years.' There are many fine images in the temples about here, but they are nearly all much too dark to take a photograph in. In one, however, I managed to get an excellent negative of a very large Buddha made of clay and gilt. In a temple close by, which is entered through a dark archway, is an elephant cast in bronze and of large size, quite as large as the tallest found in nature, and very lifelike, except that it has six tusks, three each side. This has been cast in three horizontal pieces. On his back is a huge lotus flower in which is seated a gilt image of Buddha. The whole is surrounded by a hexagonal stone palisading through which there is a doorway.

The interior of the building is very dark and is square at the base, or nearly so, changing to a circular domed roof. This was the most interesting image I saw on the mountain. The castings must be of immense weight and are undoubtedly of great age. Who the workmen were, it is, I believe, impossible to find out, and also why the figure of an elephant has been introduced, as they are unknown in the region. I have never seen an image of one before in China.

On stalls near the temple may be seen pieces of crystal for sale. These are said to come from caves in Wa-shan, and some of them contain a small quantity of water, which much increases their value. A very peculiar kind of tea is also sold, and is, I believe, only found here. When prepared for use in the ordinary way, it is very sweet without any addition of sugar. Long carved sticks are to be purchased to help one up the steep ascent, and also to take away as mementos.

The temples are very clean, and travellers are, as a rule, permitted to sleep in them on payment of a small sum. The priests generally are very civil and communicative. Wan-nien-tze itself is buried in the forest, but on the road up many beautiful views are obtained. The slopes of the mountain are clothed with pines in the upper parts, and lower down with evergreen trees of many varieties, several species of flowering currant (*Ribes*) growing in profusion underneath. Here and there a view is obtained from the head of a deep ravine, and the beauty of the scene impresses itself deeply on one's memory.

At a temple close by I left four collectors with instructions to work the whole locality, and, later on, to examine the mountain thoroughly up to the summit.

I found here a Tibetan whom I had met at Ta-tsien-lu last year, and who had come with his wife and two children to worship. The Chinese treat the Tibetans very badly, and will not permit them to use the temples to live in, but only allow them to worship there. This man, therefore, after his long journey, had to camp out with his family on the side of the mountain. He was very intelligent, and I had some conversation with him through an interpreter.

On April 12 I started for the summit, the road, generally being very winding and steep and covered in places with snow and ice. The summit was reached at 2.45 P.M., and it was bitterly cold; but this was not to be wondered at, for it is elevated 11,100 feet above the sea-level. Just before reaching the top the road passed through gloomy pine forests, and the views down the ravines to the lower spurs were very fine when the clouds below admitted.

The 'Golden Summit,' as it is called by the Chinese, has once had a magnificent temple erected on it, but this is now a mass of ruins, having been destroyed by lightning. This temple must have been constructed entirely of bronze, as there are a large number of slabs, pillars, and pieces of architraves lying about in a confused mass, all being made of that metal. In the wooden temple which has been erected close by, a few of the bronze panels have been used by being let into the walls and gilded, but all those outside seem to have no care bestowed upon them, and are left to perish. All these slabs are ornamented with the figure of Buddha, as may be seen in the illustration. There is a bronze pagoda about fifteen feet high erected on a wooden platform close to the edge of probably the highest precipice in the world. It is not much out of the perpendicular, and at least a mile in depth. The edge is guarded by rails and chains which no one is allowed to touch, but it is easy to see down. In the temple

BRONZE PAGODA AND RUINS OF BRONZE TEMPLE, SUMMIT OF MOUNT OMÉI.

there is a statuë of Buddha about fifteen feet high and closed in by curtains, many incense bowls, and other things commonly found in such places.

There were a large number of pilgrims, who worship at all the temples on the way up. Many tales are told by the priests of tigers carrying off pilgrims, who are never heard of again. All men so carried off are put down as being very wicked. I may add that if this is the case, the tigers on Mount Omêi differ very much from those in other parts of China that I have been in, for everywhere else a man-eating tiger is unknown. This mountain is considered to be the most holy in China, and many pilgrims commit suicide every year by casting themselves over the precipice.

The morning of April 13 was beautifully clear, and a splendid view was obtained from the summit. Over the clouds beneath could be seen Mount Wa to the S.S.W., while to the northward of west the snowy range above and beyond Ta-tsien-lu could be seen clearly cut against the sky. The upper surface of the clouds appeared remarkably level, and the appearance of range after range of mountains showing above them formed a magnificent spectacle. I left the summit at 10 A.M., and soon after got into mist, then rain, and, after having travelled sixty li, reached Chang-lao-ping, still on the mountain, and one of the temples of Wan-nien-tze. Here

I stayed the night. The priests differ as to the number of temples on the mountain, some saying there are sixty-four and others seventy-seven. They all agreed in giving the number of priests as 1,000, all, of course, being strict Buddhists. No life is permitted to be taken on the mountain, and before I left my collectors I saw the head priest at Wan-nien-tze, having previously seen the chief at the summit, and made them presents, also giving a subscription to keep the road in repair, getting in return permission for the collection of insects, and promising further presents on my return.

I arrived at Kia-kiang on April 15, and found my coolies waiting for me. I put up at an inn, which was very dirty and uncomfortable, but had myself to blame, for there was a much better one in the village.

Making an early start the next morning, I passed through a country well wooded, in the valley of the Ya. Much of the land is cultivated, fruit, Indian corn, and poppies being grown. The wax-producing tree is common here. I reached the village of Tsi-ko-ki in the evening, having travelled eighty li, and on April 17 much the same description of country was traversed.

On April 18 I arrived at Ya-chow at 12.30, and stayed only long enough to allow the head coolies to get their silver changed into cash. The coolies in their charge are paid at certain intervals, and there is no silver sufficiently small to pay them in; consequently, a considerable number of cash have to be carried. The quantity is always kept as small as possible because the weight is a serious matter.

Ya-chow is about 2,600 feet above the sea-level, and is a well-built city. It is a busy place, all the tea for export to Tibet being made up here into slabs. This tea is of a coarse description, and in the slabs are, besides the leaves, twigs and chopped bits of stem. The leaves are not picked, but branches are chopped from the plant and dried in the sun.

The Chinese look down upon the Tibetans, and say that this description of tea is good enough for them, but even the poorest Chinese will not use it. Tobacco is also exported to Ta-tsien-lu.

Very few junks are seen on the Ya River, the navigation being too dangerous, but goods are sent down in long narrow bamboo rafts. Many of these come up loaded with *samshew* (native spirit) in large earthenware jars, holding perhaps fifty gallons each and cased in bamboo. These are stowed in a single line right along the centre of the raft, which may carry as many as thirty, and are brought from Sui-fu.

Passing through Ya-chow, the village of Tzu-shih-li was reached in the evening. Here the valley of the Ya, through which we had travelled for the last three days, crossing the river six times, comes to an end, and the mountainous region commences. The weather was very hot, and my Tibetan dog, Ja-ma, was so knocked up that I was obliged to have him carried in a chair by two coolies.

On April 19 the road led up the rocky bed of a small stream for fifteen li, the ground rising till an altitude of 4,500 feet was attained. Yung-ching-hsien was reached in the evening, and here my Yamen runners were changed. Just before reaching the town a small river had to be crossed. There is a large quantity of iron manufactured in this place. The pans for the evaporation of brine are cast, and many smaller articles are produced both in cast and wrought iron. Going out the following day by the west gate of the city, I passed through a whole street of blacksmiths, and reached Huang-ni-pu, 3,600 feet above the sea, at 3.30, having travelled fifty li.

On the 21st the coolies struck work. They said that they were too tired to go any further, and that the roads had been very bad. They certainly had been hard-worked, but not more so than they are accustomed to. However, as there was no official in the place to appeal to, I was forced to grant a day's rest, and the time was spent by them in idleness and opium-smoking.

The next day, April 22, a start was made without

any trouble, and the ascent of the pass Tai-hsiang-ling-kwan, 9,270 feet above the sea, was made. From the top of the pass there is a fine view of the snowy ranges to the westward. Ching-chi-hsien, at an elevation of 4,750 feet, was seen down below, and reached in the evening. It is notorious for high winds, and on this occasion its character was well kept up, for it blew a gale and was a particularly stormy night. I found a good inn, and the officials were civil.

On April 23, after a very fatiguing march over bad and stony roads on a very hot day, I reached Ni-tou in the evening. This place lies at the head of a very deep and stony ravine. The ground is much cut up by small watercourses, which occur in great numbers, leading off the slopes of the mountains into the ravine. In spite of the stony nature of the surface there is much vegetation, and I subsequently had a collector here. I joined the road traversed the previous year at Fu-chuang. The Fei-yueh-ling Pass was reached at 2.30 the next day, and at the summit I found a very fine mauve primula in bloom. I reached Hua-lin-ping in the evening and stopped for the night.

Lu-ting-chiao was passed through on April 25, and I went on to Cha-pa, where I was most kindly received again by the missionaries, with whom I stayed for the night. It was a hard and dangerous march, the road having been destroyed by landslips in many places since I last passed.

On April 27 I reached Ta-tsien-lu for the second time. Before reaching the city gates, I got a letter from Bishop Biet telling me that a report had been spread in the place that Mr. Kricheldorff and myself were two foreign mandarins, and that he expected I might have trouble with the authorities. However, on producing our passports we were allowed to enter without any opposition. I found that a new mandarin had been appointed since my last visit, who was much prejudiced against foreigners and not so easy to get on with.

I found accommodation at the same inn I had stayed at before, and was very busy for the next few days paying off coolies, telling off collectors, and unpacking and distributing apparatus.

CHAPTER XIII

TA-TSIEN-LU

Excursion to the south-east—Camp at an altitude of 12,500 feet—Rhododendron logs—*Crossoptilon*—Snow and frost—Search for road—Lake discovered—Salamanders—Mr. Kricheldorff goes to Mou-pin—Execution of Tibetans—Oppression of lamas—Message from Tibetan king—Try to find plateau to the north—Larvæ and pupa of *Parnassius imperator*—Departure for neighbourhood of Mo-si-mien—Musk deer—Local king's palace—Ponies and cattle—Meet Tibetan king—King's farm—Hot springs—Pheasants and *Ithaginis*—Mo-si-mien Pass—Ya-chow-kun—Medicine collectors—Camping-ground chosen—Log hut—Lake discovered—Trip to Ta-tsien-lu—Snow-storm—Fine trees to the southward—Pu-tzu-fong—Black currants and small fruits—Natives excited against foreigner—Collectors at Ni-tou—Return to Ta-tsien-lu—Petition against my return south—Arrival of caravan from Shi-ga-tze—Père Jeridot—Arrival of Prince Henri of Orleans—His collections—Races—Disturbance in city—Robbery—Breeding *Crossoptilon*—*Lophophorus L'huysii*—Tragopan—Parrots—Eagles.

I FOUND the same missionaries that were here last year, and they were most kind in every way and of great assistance to me, Bishop Biet very kindly cashing my cheques.

On May 1 I left for a trip to the snowy mountains to the south-east of Ta-tsien-lu, taking nine men and a good tent with me. Leaving the town by the south gate the path led up a rocky ravine, and up to an altitude of

4,000 feet dwarf pink azaleas and anemones were particularly noticeable among many varieties of flowers. Above this rhododendrons grew in the greatest abundance and of large size, many stems being over a foot in diameter. Their flowers were large and of many shades of colour, and their limit was about 12,000 feet above the level of the sea. I also saw many fine varieties of primula growing among the rhododendrons. The tent was pitched at an altitude of 12,500 feet, and some time was spent before a sufficiently level piece of ground could be found. Our fuel was logs of the largest rhododendrons, and a good fire had to be kept up, for though we were in a sheltered place it was very cold directly the sun went down. *Crossoptilon* appeared to be abundant; I saw a great many feeding on the rocky slopes of the spurs and also heard them calling, which they invariably do at early dawn and dusk, thus betraying their presence.

During the night there was a fall of snow and a severe frost. I find that I am about two hours' journey from the line of perpetual snow and glaciers. The days are hot but the nights intensely cold. There are no inhabitants within some miles. Father Soulié arrived on the evening of May 2, and on the following day we ascended, to find, if possible, a suitable camping-place higher up, and also to see if a road could be found, leading to the southward, through the pine forest that grows there, by which I might travel in the direction of Mo-si-mien without getting onto the regular track. This I was anxious to do if possible, as I should thereby avoid any contact with the lamas, who were, I knew, inclined to be troublesome, and who are found in swarms on the roads near Ta-tsien-lu. Unfortunately I could find no road, the southern slopes being covered with virgin forests of pine which I was unable to penetrate.

I discovered during the day a lovely lake of the clearest and purest water, and very deep. On the banks quantities of sulphur were lying. It was surrounded on all sides except the north by precipices many hundreds of feet deep, and had the appearance of receiving the overflow of a lake above by a waterfall at the south end. I can only conjecture the presence of such a lake, but the formation seemed strongly to indicate it. Its elevation I made to be 14,070 feet above the sea, and its overflow supplies a tributary of the river flowing through Ta-tsien-lu. It took me two hours to walk round, so that a rough idea may be formed of its size. At the north end were a number of Tibetan prayer-sticks, with thin strings and papers fluttering in the wind. I saw some salamanders in the lake, and on the precipices round it were some birds much resembling the chough.

It was a beautiful place, and a splendid view was obtained to the northward. I much regretted that I had not got my camera with me on this occasion—the only time I ever was there.

On May 4, leaving the tent and my men on the mountain, I returned to Ta-tsien-lu in order to despatch Mr. Kricheldorff to Mou-pin, a place, ten days' journey to the E.N.E. of Ta-tsien-lu, which is but little known, Père David and another French missionary being, I believe, the only Europeans that have ever visited it. I gave him directions to establish at least four stations, and sent a cook and interpreter and six collectors with him, fitting him out with a good tent, as I was nearly sure he could find no houses to live in.

Before this, on my entering the town by the south gate, I saw five Tibetan heads hanging in bamboo cages. These, I learned, belonged to five men who had been executed near Litang while I was away. The frontier seemed to be in a very unsettled state, and I was told that on the military mandarin hearing of a disturbance, he promptly proceeded to the place and had these five men, whom he considered to be the ring-leaders, beheaded at once. One of the heads had belonged apparently to a mere lad of about sixteen or seventeen. After they had been exposed here for a certain time, they would be sent on to Cheng-tu as a warning, and also to show that the sentence had been carried out, Cheng-tu being the capital of Sze-chuen.

The people here appeared to be much oppressed and ground down by the lamas. These worthies form a very considerable proportion of the population and do no work at all. They, however, lend money to the agriculturists when they can, at ruinous rates of interest, the result being that in most cases the whole of the unfortunate borrower's property falls into their hands, or rather into the hands of the principals of the lamaseries to which they belong. As a natural consequence these are nearly all very wealthy. The people are also heavily taxed upon every sort of property, and are so poor as to be hardly able to live.

I returned to my camp on May 7 and made another attempt to find a way to the south, but failed; and then moved my tent higher up on the mountain, pitching it at an elevation of 13,000 feet. The next day I received a message from the Tibetan king forbidding me to remain camped on the mountain, as it is a sacred reservation; but before leaving I determined to try again for a pass southward, and was again disappointed. My coolies also were sent out, but they too failed to find any way higher up the mountain, as there was so much snow. The tent was pitched at the head of a valley, the sides of which could be seen for miles down covered with rhododendrons in blossom of all shades of white, pink, and red—a perfect sea of bloom. On May 10 I felt obliged to comply with the directions contained in the king's message, and returned to Ta-tsien-lu.

Having heard of a plateau to the north, about a day's journey from the town, where plenty of game was to be found, I left to try and reach it on May 12; but after a hard day's march I found that I had been misinformed, and a Christian guide told me that such a place as I was in search of existed four days' journey away. I had no time, however, to proceed further, and I had reached an elevation of 14,000 feet. The mountains were covered where possible by pine forests; but the surface was very rocky, and there were a number of isolated sugar-loaf shaped rocks to be seen, some being quite 1,000 feet high. On the ridges, slightly lower, rhododendrons were interspersed with various other bushes.

I saw no signs of any inhabitants, and I found, among other interesting plants, a large terrestrial orchid from seven to eight feet high, bearing several broad opposite leaves on the stem, and at the top a loose spike of inconspicuous flowers, small and of a greenish-purple colour; and a plant that reminded me of a gigantic marsh marigold, the lower leaves being quite two feet in diameter,

RHODODENDRONS. ALTITUDE 12,000 FEET.

and the flower stem over four feet high and at least four inches in diameter. The flowers were yellow and about two inches across.

On the 13th I returned to Ta-tsien-lu and then prepared for a journey to Mo-si-mien, where I intended to stay, if possible, for the summer. I found time to search for the larvæ of *Parnassius imperator* and got about twenty, and one pupa. The larva is found on a species of umbelliferous plant and is of a dark slate colour, with ten orange spots on each side, each spot with a black rim. It is covered with short grey hairs, and when touched curls itself into a ring. Its length is 1⅜ inch. The pupa is brown, and is found attached by a silk web to the under surface of stones.

On May 15, having made all arrangements, I left Ta-tsien-lu for the neighbourhood of Mo-si-mien, having fourteen coolies carrying my apparatus and a tent. Leaving the town by the south gate, the road passes up a valley, the west side of which is covered with pine forest and is strictly preserved by the king. Many musk deer are trapped in it, and the sale of the musk they yield forms a considerable part of his income. He allows no timber to be cut in it. Further on the mountains are rocky and barren, or nearly so.

At a distance of about twenty li from Ta-tsien-lu the palace of the local king is situated. This is a large, rambling sort of place, with walls of mud and a Chinese tiled roof. It is built partly over a natural hot spring, which may be seen running away from the foundations, the steam passing out by the eaves of a part of the palace. Close by is a large farm, where I noticed many very good-looking ponies and a large number of cows. These are kept for milking, and are of a much superior class to those usually seen about the country, resembling the Alderney in appearance, but rather larger and coarser. I also saw about twenty elk, all females, in an enclosure. There was plenty of capital grass-feed about the place, principally on the smaller plateaux which abound in the neighbourhood. Besides being a large farmer and horse breeder, the king is a great sportsman, and when I met him close to his farm he had a pack of hounds at his heels. He is an elderly man and does not enjoy good health, but is a great believer in the virtues of the various hot springs which abound in the neighbourhood, from one of which he was returning when I met him. He was dressed in the usual costume of the Tibetans of the better class, and had a huge scarlet umbrella carried over his head by his attendants. On seeing me he stopped and wished to enter into conversation, which was accomplished by my cook acting as interpreter.

He told me that he had never heard of my arrival. This did not exactly agree with the message I had received when on the mountain some days before, and I never was able to find out whether he was telling a falsehood or whether my men had invented the message said to have come from him. I strongly suspect, however, that his royal memory was rather short. He was much interested in the gun I was carrying (an ordinary 12-bore double), and wanted to know how far it would kill. He seemed to be an intelligent man, well informed considering the country in which he lived, and he had been to Pekin. He is a practically independent chieftain, but sends tribute once in two years to Pekin, and has frequent disputes as to questions of jurisdiction with the Chinese officials at Ta-tsien-lu. He is wealthy, as things go there, his riches being principally in land, cattle, and ponies, owning several hundreds of the latter.

About ten li further on I reached a Tibetan hamlet, being, in fact, one of his dairy-farms, where I slept in a house owned by his Majesty, and I was lucky enough to get delicious milk and butter, though the place was rather dirty. The house was built in the Tibetan fashion, of loose stones, clay being used to fill the interstices, the roof being shingled with long split-pine shingles upon which were placed large stones to prevent the high winds, so prevalent here, blowing them off. Here there are three hot springs, each issuing from the top of a yellowish-brown conical rock. These cones have evidently been formed by the continued incrustation of the minerals contained in the water, the largest being about fifteen feet high, and the other two slightly less. The water issuing from them is very hot, and has a very offensive odour, resembling decaying sea-weed. The three springs unite and form a stream, which runs through the valley, a black slime accumulating on its edges in which green aquatic plants grow even when the water is still quite warm. The king has a wooden bath built round with stones here, and it is filled by means of a bamboo pipe leading to the top of one of the cones.

Starting early the next morning (May 16) the ascent became more steep, and the stunted vegetation and scarcity of even pines soon showed, if there were no other indications, that a high elevation was being reached. Small grassy plateaux, however, were frequent, and the Tibetan pheasant (*Phasianus decollatus*) appeared to be very common. I shot several, and noticed also that a species of *Ithaginis* was very common, as they were constantly running across the path. They are, however, of not much use for food, being very tough and having an unpleasantly strong flavour. Just before reaching the summit of the pass I noticed a very beautiful dwarf blue iris, and a little higher up I found patches of snow. It was bitterly cold, and on reaching

VIEW FROM MO-SI-MIEN PASS, LOOKING WEST.

the top I made the elevation to be 12,800 feet above sea-level. Every winter lives are lost in this pass, for though poles are put up to mark the track, if a snow-storm should come on it is very easy to lose the way, the pass not being just a passage over a ridge, but the road leads right across a depression about three miles across, called by the coolies, 'the cup.' Any deviation from the path here would put them in deep snow, from which they could only with the greatest difficulty extricate themselves. On commencing the descent, in most disagreeable weather, snow and sleet falling heavily, I was glad to reach after a time a place named Ya-chow-kun, where there is a rest-house frequented principally by the Chinese collectors of medicine. There were nearly fifty of them when I arrived, and a huge fire was burning in the middle of the place, fed with logs quite two feet in diameter. There was no chimney and the inside was black with smoke; the heat was, however, very comforting, and I found that there was a small room built off at one end which I appropriated to my own use. The house, though built strongly and on a level piece of ground, had been blown much out of the perpendicular, and had it not been supported by struts on one side would certainly have fallen. The principal room was about sixty feet long by thirty broad, and in it the medicine collectors lived and slept. Just outside the door was a nauseating heap of all manner of filth, the accumulation of years. The medicines collected here are rhubarb, *Tchöng-tsaö* (*Sphæria sinensis*), a plant the root of which bears an almost exact resemblance to the body of a caterpillar, and *pey-mou* (*Fritillaria Roylii*), a small bulb about the size of a marble, to which tonic principles are attributed.

The next day I started to find a suitable place for camping in the neighbourhood, and after having crossed a small stream opposite the house by means of a log bridge, I found a path gradually ascending through virgin pine forest, ending at last at an abandoned clearing about twenty li from Ya-chow-kun. I saw at once that it was a very suitable place for camping, and I especially wanted a clear place in order to be able to sugar at night for moths. Near by was a small lake, the banks of which were clothed with rhododendrons. The pine trees round had a beautiful lichen growing on them of a pea-green colour, which hung from the limbs and branches in graceful festoons. The elevation was 12,000 feet above the sea. I sent back and had all my baggage brought up, the tent being pitched as soon as possible. The climate being very damp, I saw that it would be almost impossible to preserve specimens unless a house was built, and I set my men to work to erect one the day following. It was built of logs after

CAMP ON SITE OF LOG HUT.

the manner of the log huts of North America, the smaller trees being cut down and notched near the ends, which are then fitted over one another. One side was built higher than the other, so as to have a lean-to roof with a good slope. This, being well covered with split-pine shingles, kept the wet out perfectly. I even went so far as to have glass windows made out of spoilt photographic plates; and I insisted on having a wooden chimney built, though my men were very averse to it and wished to have the room always full of smoke and allow it to escape as it best could through the roof. This hut was about twenty feet by fifteen feet, and was, when finished, very comfortable. It took about a fortnight to complete, and then a fire was kept burning day and night drying botanical papers and specimens.

On the lake I noticed some yellow ducks of the same species that is common on the Yang-tze, and in the forest there was a woodpecker, speckled black and white with a red crest. I saw but few butterflies, the weather being so cold, and those were mostly of the genus *Pieris*.

On May 20 I went out in a north-easterly direction, and ascended to an elevation of 15,200 feet above the sea. I found a lake at this altitude, and collected a good many beetles from under the stones. I was rather surprised to find them in such numbers so close to the line of perpetual snow. About here is a great place for the medicine collectors, and I found a fine species of wild onion of good flavour growing in moist ground. There were also many lilies of various species, but none in bloom. I took some photographs from this place.

One night I noticed that the tent was leaking through the drip from a pine tree falling on it, and I told a coolie to cut it down and to be sure to have a rope made fast to clear it of the tent in its fall. He cut the tree down but took no precaution, the consequence being that it fell right across the ridge pole, and had it not been for a tree on the other side, against which it fell, everything in the tent must have been smashed. As it was, a good deal of damage was done; but I only mention this to show how careless these people are.

On May 23 I received a letter from Father Soulié, telling me that two of my collectors had come in from Wa-ssu-kou, and were in want of more collecting boxes and a larger cyanide bottle. I was, therefore, obliged to return to Ta-tsien-lu to see to their requirements. Crossing the pass, the weather being fine and clear, splendid views were obtained both to the south, over the forest-clad valley as far as the eye could reach beyond Mo-si-mien, and to the north, as far as the snow-clad mountains beyond Ta-tsien-lu. To the left was a conical-shaped mountain covered with snow—a most conspicuous object. Descending to the valley small plateaux are constantly passed, covered with rich grass in which many buttercups are seen.

Having given the collectors what they required, I started southward again on May 25, and slept that night at the dairy-farm I had before visited. I was somewhat disconcerted at finding that a very dirty lama was to share the only room with me, but there was no choice. He was very busy chanting prayers (the only thing they ever do), and his accent seemed to remind me of Italian.

Leaving at daylight I had a stiff walk to the top of the pass, and just after passing the summit I came to a horse, evidently just dead, lying on the path with a bridle on. I could never find out who his owner had been or how he came there, but I strongly suspect that there had been foul play. I reached camp in the evening, and during the night there was a heavy storm of thunder and lightning accompanied by hail and snow.

May 31.—Snowing very fast, the ground covered and the branches of the trees loaded with snow, looking much more like midwinter than three weeks from midsummer.

The first of June was a fine day, but the snow lay thick on the ground and light fleecy clouds floated in the air. I managed to ascend to about 15,000 feet, and collected in the sheltered spots some beetles from under the stones. Next day I collected a few butterflies.

June 3.—I took a walk of about twenty-five li to the southward. The path led through a forest of magnificent pine trees as straight as an arrow, many being three feet in diameter. They would make splendid timber if there was any use for it in the place where it grows, but there are no roads or means of transporting such large trunks. In places the rhododendrons were very beautiful, and grow larger than at the higher elevations. Oak trees, several species of beech, larch, limes, walnut, stunted bamboo, and many evergreens are also plentiful. The bark of the pines was covered with lichen and ferns. I returned to camp in the evening.

June 5.—A heavy snow-storm and bitterly cold, all the bloom being cut off the rhododendrons. Really terrible weather, and like a Canadian winter. In the evening there was a foot of snow on the ground. A coolie came in during the day with the news that the road to Ta-tsien-lu was blocked with snow, and that the people at Mo-si-mien, having heard from the medicine collectors that there was a foreigner residing in the district, attributed the severe weather to his presence. They being much lower down the valley had heavy sleet-storms instead of snow.

LOG HUT ON JUNE 5, 1890.

The coolie also told me that the horse that had been killed near the top of the pass had been almost entirely devoured by leopards.

The snow-storm continued till June 9, on which day there was a rapid thaw. Before this set in there were three feet of snow on the ground, and on the 12th, the weather appearing to be more settled, I made a trip to the southward, and, again passing through the forest, I crossed a tributary of the Tung River by a wooden bridge at Ta-chiao 8,000 feet above the sea. Even at this lower elevation there were not many species of lepidoptera out yet, the recent snow-storm having doubtless retarded their appearance. I arrived at Pu-tzu-fong in the evening, where there is a hut which gives a bare shelter, but not much more, to the medicine collectors who frequent the neighbourhood.

This appeared to be a very favourable spot for collecting later on—probably next month would be a very good time—and I resolved to have a station here. I therefore left the botanical collector with directions to gather specimens of plants during the day and to sugar for moths at night. He had two men under his orders for day-work with the lepidoptera.

On my way to this place I noticed some black currant bushes, which grew to a height of nearly eighteen feet, bearing bunches of fruit at least a foot long, the berries being about the size of the ordinary black currant and having a fair flavour. They were borne thinly on the bunches, and the whole plant had the peculiar odour of the common kind.

A species of dwarf rubus, about six inches high and bearing a single yellow berry of excellent flavour, was common, the fruit being often eaten by my coolies and myself when on the march. They are also gathered by the Tibetan women and sold at Ta-tsien-lu. Wild strawberries and small wild gooseberries of no value were also common.

While at Pu-tzu-fong I heard that all sorts of rumours were abroad about my presence being the cause of the severe weather, and that the inhabitants of Mo-si-mien were so excited on the subject, and so furious with me, that it would be unsafe to visit the place. I had therefore reluctantly to abandon my project of seeing it, and the next day I returned to Celestial Cottage, as I called my hut on the hills.

Before making the trip just mentioned, I had sent two collectors down to Pu-tzu-fong, one being a capital man whom I thought I could trust. He was pilot of my boat, and had the year before done very well indeed, collecting at Chin-kou-ho. After ten days' stay, however, they came back, saying that the natives would not allow them to collect, but that they knew of a place where splendid collections could be made. I allowed them to go, giving them the necessary money and apparatus. Some little time afterwards I heard that they had tramped all the way back to Ni-tou, where they were spending their time and my money in opium-smoking, there being also a further attraction in the shape of a Chinese damsel. Of course I recalled them immediately, but it was most annoying to have the valuable time so wasted.

On June 14 I noticed that the medicine collectors were all absent, instead of being scattered over the hills as usual. This, together with what my men had told me, looked suspicious, so I decided to go to Ta-tsien-lu and see the magistrate, as perhaps he might be able to make things go more smoothly. Leaving camp at noon, I crossed the pass, and on the north side, at an elevation of 10,000 feet, and where the ground had lately been covered with snow, I found a plant in bloom much resembling a gloxinia, the flower being crimson.

I reached the city in the evening and went to the inn, where I found quarters.

On June 17 the mandarin received a despatch at 9 P.M., which he sent on to Mgr. Biet, from whom I heard the contents. It was a petition from Mo-si-mien, signed by a large number of the inhabitants, and also by the medicine collectors, who had left the hills foı the purpose, stating that my presence had caused the severe weather lately prevalent, and requesting that I might be ordered to leave the district at once. It seemed to be a curious exhibition of ignorance and superstition; but the mandarin had no friendly feelings towards foreigners, so that it was useless to try to live in the hut any longer, the mandarin refusing to allow me to remain long out of the city. I had, however, gained some knowledge of the country, and could send my men to any places that I considered likely, as the natives raised no objections to their living and collecting where-ever they were sent.

On June 19 the annual caravan arrived from Shi-ga-tze, near the frontier of Sikkim and the capital of the province of Tishulumbo, the town being now crowded with Tibetans. This caravan travels by the way of Tsiamdo, this route being chosen as it affords sufficient pasture for the large number of animals that are made use of. They consist of horses and the cross-bred animal between a yak and a cow. I could form no idea of the number employed as the greater part were in camp, some being miles away from the city. This is necessary in order to get sufficient feed. They bring quantities of goods, principally narrow, striped woollen cloth, and very thick woollen rugs, which are much used for saddle-cloths. The colours are green, red, and yellow

PART OF SHI-GA-TZE CARAVAN ENCAMPED OUTSIDE LAMASSERY.

of subdued shades. The caravan usually stays about a month, and they take back Ya-chow brick tea in exchange for their goods. The journey from Shi-ga-tze takes five months. They brought news that a French prince, with several Europeans and a strong escort, had arrived at Batang on his way to this city.

A few days later I had a message from Mgr. Biet that a European had arrived from Tungalow, three days' journey west. On going to the palace, I found Père Jeridot, who seemed from his emaciated appearance to have led a life of great privation. With the exception of the Fathers here, he had not seen a European for thirteen years. He spoke a little English with an excellent pronunciation, but told me that he had forgotten most of the language. From Tungalow there is hardly any communication even with this place, and all letters have to be sent secretly by means of converts who trade between the two places.

Originally he was at Batang, but the mission buildings were burned by the Tibetans, and everything, including a valuable library, destroyed. He and another Father had to return to Ta-tsien-lu, and after some time got a promise of indemnity from the Chinese Government, which, however, has never been paid, there being a dispute as to who were liable to pay, the Chinese or the Tibetans. They then got a pass permitting them to return to Batang, but were stopped at Tungalow by the military mandarin, who refused to allow them to proceed any further. They, however, declined to return, and established a mission there.

Mgr. Biet tells me that there is a missionary living near the frontier of Yunnan who, unless he saw Mr. Cooper when he passed through, has seen no European, with the exception of a brother missionary now and then, at long intervals, for the last thirty years.

June 24.—Prince Henri of Orleans arrived from Litang and took up his quarters at the inn I was staying at. He had travelled right across Tibet from Kuldja by way of Lob nor, Tengri nor and Batang, having been close to Lhassa, which city he was unable to enter. He was accompanied by two Europeans, Messrs. Bonvalot and De' Deken, the latter belonging to the Belgian mission in Mongolia, and who spoke the Chinese language fluently. He had a large number of followers and pack animals, having made large natural history collections on the journey. Though, as I said before, he was unable to enter Lhassa, he received a very valuable present from the Grand Lama which was sent out of the city to him.

The next day Mgr. Biet had a dinner party, to which I was invited. I found Père Jeridot and Fathers Dejean and Soulié, Prince Henri, Messrs.

Bonvalot and De' Deken, a party of eight Europeans, certainly the largest number ever assembled before at Ta-tsien-lu. Prince Henri informed me that he and his party had suffered severe hardships on their journey. The cold in the high and previously unexplored passes between Lob nor and Tengri nor was intense, and he had lost two men from the combined effects of frost-bites and the rarified condition of the atmosphere. He had taken ten months in crossing from Kuldja, and, together with the whole of his party, was much fatigued by his long journey. The next day he showed me some of the skins he had collected. Among them was one of a magnificent yak, and several of bears and antelopes. He had also the head of a white antelope with spiral horns, probably a new species. He had camels as far as Lob nor, from which place he despatched home, by way of Kuldja, the collections already made.

June 29.—Great excitement in the town to-day, as the Tibetan king has his annual race meeting. These races begin early in the morning, between five and six o'clock, and last all day. The riders are boys, who wear distinguishing colours as in more civilised countries. The start is made on the hills above the town—perhaps a thousand feet higher—and the boys and ponies race down the steep descent and through the town as hard as they can go. All the inhabitants of the city turn out to look on, the races being one of the great events of the year. The king, I was informed, gave three prizes, but the racing went on all day, a large number of ponies being made use of.

July 2.—Yesterday Prince Henri sent his interpreter (Mons. De' Deken) to the Yamen, with a request to see the mandarin. The mandarin refused to grant an interview, and upon the request being repeated, again declined. He then spread a report that the interpreter had come to the Yamen for the purpose of robbing the treasury. This, of course, caused great excitement among the lamas and inhabitants, which was increased when it became known that he (the mandarin) had sent to the military mandarin for soldiers to arrest the Europeans. This the military mandarin refused to do, and the Tibetan king being applied to for the same purpose, also refused to send any men, saying that he did not believe it and that the mandarin was a liar. The king was always on bad terms with the mandarin, and to find him without support from the military authorities was exactly what he wanted.

Things, however, began to look very queer and I did not know how they were going to turn out. A mob had collected, and they are in China always dangerous. A trifle might incense them against the foreigners and cause a general attack to be made. In the evening things quieted down a little, and on July 3 it was reported that the mandarin had sent a courier to Cheng-tu for instructions. The missionaries tell me that they have never known such anxious times. The people appear to have become quieter. Had this mob assembled at places like Chung-king or Kia-ting-fu, all the foreigners would probably have been massacred, but here the people are all traders and more peaceably inclined.

July 16.—Last night Prince Henri was robbed of silver to the value of 300 taels, and various other articles, the thieves effecting an entrance by a window after having climbed over the wall of the inn courtyard. The mandarin, on being informed of the theft, acted in a very half-hearted manner, and none of the stolen property was recovered. The Prince had no passport, and therefore no responsibility rested with the mandarin. If he had been properly provided with one, the former trouble would probably not have arisen.

Soon after I arrived at Ta-tsien-lu I found that, by taking trouble, I could procure eggs of the *Crossoptilon Tibetanum*, and I thought that by getting these hatched out under fowls, I might be able to take some young birds of this remarkably fine species home, considering that they were well-adapted for acclimatization in a European country. I accordingly sent out collectors to the most likely places, and they brought in at different times about a hundred eggs, which are of a light olive dun colour. Broody hens were procured, not without difficulty, and these, with clutches of eggs, were distributed among such of the native converts as had suitable places for rearing the young birds. The heathen natives could not be trusted with such things, being much more rough and less reliable. In the end I got a good percentage hatched out, and fifty-three were alive at Kia-ting-fu, having been carried down from Ta-tsien-lu by coolies. Being so young, the journey was too severe, and many were in a bad state of health from the overland journey. Losses were heavy going down the river, and I only succeeded in getting five home alive. I put this heavy mortality down to the birds being too young to travel. If I could have left them till the next year, I feel confident I should have succeeded in bringing nearly all home alive. The year before, Mgr. Biet gave me an adult specimen that had been hatched and reared in his aviary, and this bird stood the passage perfectly well. It is, with the others I brought home, now in the gardens of the Royal Zoological Society, Regent's Park.

Another bird, a specimen of which I brought home alive, is the *Lophophorus L'huysii*. This magnificent species inhabits high altitudes near the snow line, and has never before been brought alive to Europe. They are

HAUNTS OF THE *LOPHOPHORUS L'HUYSII* AND *CROSSOPTILON TIBETANUM.*
Altitude of Camera, 13,520 feet.

by no means common or easy to find, but when once seen do not appear to be at all timid and may be approached to within a few feet. Two were brought me, having been snared by the leg near Wan-Tung, in the mountains; one, unfortunately, died, but the other travelled home safely, and is now in the Zoological Society's gardens. I tried to procure their eggs but failed, natives bringing me eggs of *Ithaginis*, which they assured me were those of the *Lophophorus*; but, luckily, I had found the nest of the *Ithaginis* myself, and could easily recognise their cream-coloured eggs thickly sprinkled with small spots of brown, and I was not, therefore, to be taken in.

These birds are very fond of the small peymou bulb, and, in places where it is plentiful, scratch it out of the soil. The natives, if they find a place much used, and where a fair quantity of the bulbs still remain, set a number of nooses pegged down and frequently capture the birds by the leg.

Some adult *Crossoptilon* that had been snared were brought to me alive, but these all died. They roost in large companies in the forest, and if a native finds a roosting-place and has a gun, he lights a fire underneath, and can then shoot every bird singly, they appearing to be dazed by the light of the fire, and taking no notice of the report of the gun.

In the winter these birds come much lower down in search of food, and are easier of approach.

The tragopan (*Ceriornis temminki*) is found in the district, but is not often seen, as it inhabits the almost impenetrable pine forest. I brought home a specimen alive that I purchased from a native who had caught it. Monkeys are seen in troops in the Mo-si-mien forest, and Mgr. Biet informed me that a very large monkey or ape occurs in the mountains of South Tibet, and that it is probably a new species.

Prince Henri had specimens of a green parrot which he found to be very numerous at Batang. As this is in nearly 30° N. Lat., I should think it was the furthest north that they are found. Father Soulié, who has been there, tells me that they fly about very plentifully in the suburbs.

In an excursion north of Ta-tsien-lu, I noticed an eagle's nest among the cliffs which evidently contained young birds. It was in a very precipitous place and absolutely unapproachable. Vultures may be commonly seen soaring among the mountains. The way in which they sail in the air for hours together, with but seldom any apparent motion of the wings, is very remarkable.

CHAPTER XIV

MOUNT OMÊI

Prepare to leave Ta-tsien-lu—Take charge of Prince Henri's collection—Collectors left behind—Departure—Village destroyed by landslip—Lu-ting-chiao—Sick woman—New road—Pass Chih-pan-kow, Fung-ya-ping and San-yan-kwan—Arrive at Yo-so-po—Tai-hsiang-ling-kwan Pass—Huang-ni-po—Shih-chia-chiao—Ya-chow-fu—Orders to travel by Hung-ya-hsien—Heavy rain—Robbery at Tsi-ho-kia—Hung-ya-hsien—Landlord in trouble—Kia-kiang—Kia-ting-fu—Depart for Omêi-shan—Wan-nien-ssu—Summit of Mount Omêi—Glory of Buddha—Temples easily destroyed by fire—Quantity of bronze on mountain—Iron suspension bridges.

July 18.—Finding that I could do nothing more in Ta-tsien-lu, as my movements were so hampered by the mandarin, who, though everything was now perfectly quiet, refused to allow me to return to my log cabin, I determined to leave and make a stay on Mount Omêi, where I was anxious to see how my men were getting on. Prince Henri of Orleans had determined to return by way of Yunnan to Hanoi, and as by this route he would have greater difficulty in transporting his collection of natural history specimens than by the river route to Shanghai, he asked me to take charge of them as far as Hankow, at which place he wished them given over to the French Consul. Upon my deciding to take them, he sent me eighteen coolie loads. These, with twenty coolie loads of my own, formed the total that I started with. I was now very busy packing up all the collections and getting in those from the stations outside the town. My collectors had orders to leave a month after I had gone, bring all they had found with them, and meet me at Kia-ting-fu. I also sent two men to a place called Ho-kow, ten days' journey west of Ta-tsien-lu, on the road, and about half way to Litang, which is situated in a valley nearly surrounded by lofty plateaux, where I expected they would find some interesting and rare insects.

Many of my boxes were covered with raw hide by the Tibetans, who are very expert at this work. They take a hide from a freshly killed animal and fit and sew this over the boxes in a particularly neat way with the hair inside. When the hide dries, it shrinks and hardens, forming a splendid and almost indestructible covering.

July 21.—All being ready, I left Ta-tsien-lu after having thanked Mgr. Biet and the Fathers for their kindness and said good-bye, and arrived at Wa-ssu-kou in the evening.

July 22.—A village was passed to-day situated on the side of a valley near the banks of the Tung, which had

VIEW FROM SITE OF LOG HUT, LOOKING NORTH.

been nearly destroyed by a landslip, or, rather, mudslip, since my last journey through. Quite half the houses had been utterly destroyed, and many of those remaining were filled with a deposit of mud and stones. It may seem difficult to understand how these houses are thus filled with rubbish, because one would be apt to think they would be thrown down; but the Chinese build their houses in a different manner to what we are accustomed to see, for they first get uprights of timber fixed in the ground, upon which plates are laid and the roof is built upon them. Then the walls are built between the uprights, and are composed of stone, brick, or mud, according to the locality and the means of the builder. When a flood or a landslip occurs and reaches a house so built, the first thing to go is one of the walls, and if they are not all demolished, a large deposit takes place, naturally, within the building. On my journey westward a hill had to be descended, here a dry watercourse was crossed by a bridge, and an ascent made on the other side. Now there was a nearly level road across, and the bridge was either swept away or buried. Hundreds of acres of level and cultivated ground had been covered with earth and stones to a depth of seven or eight feet, and all the crops destroyed. What had been a scene of prosperity was now one of desolation, and the mischief had probably been caused by the sudden melting of the snow above, which had lain much later than usual on account of the severity of the weather. When the warmth came and caused a sudden thaw, the water thus freed brought the earth and stones down. The Tung River had evidently been quite lately much swollen, but was now lower.

The mail man from Chung-king to Ta-tsien-lu was passed to-day, and though I felt certain that there were letters for me, I could not get them as they were in a sealed packet directed to Mgr. Biet.

Lu-ting-chiao was reached in the evening, and here my escort was changed, those that had accompanied me going back to Ta-tsien-lu and others coming on as far as Chin-chi-hsien.

July 23.—The road travelled over to-day was in a very bad state, much damage having been done by the late rains. This, however, is nothing more than what one may expect where the roads are mere tracks that are only kept open at all by the traffic that passes along. As a rule, no attempt is made to form what we should consider to be a road. Arrived at Hua-ling-ping in the evening, the coolies arriving much later, having had a hard day's work.

July 24.—To-day, when on the march, I met a man and woman, the latter evidently seriously ill, apparently suffering from dysentery. I could do nothing except give her a dose of chlorodyne, which I thought might do her good. They both appeared to be very grateful for the medicine. In the evening Ni-tou was reached.

July 25.—After two hours' march, I left the road by which I had travelled before, and turning to the left passed up a fine open valley and through highly cultivated land. The surface was rolling, the soil evidently very fertile and of a red colour, with granite boulders cropping up in places. Much Indian corn was growing, and clumps of walnut trees were plentiful. The road was gradually ascending, and the summit of a ridge 6,500 feet above the sea was reached at 10 A.M. Descending at first by a road that was trying in places, the village of Chih-pan-kow was reached and a short halt made. Then passing through Chih-pan-kow and Fung-ya-ping, both villages, the road ascended again till a second ridge was reached, called San-yan-kwan, 7,350 feet above the sea. From here I descended to Yo-so-po (6,250 feet), where I intended to stay the night. Chin-chi-hsien is seen from here, being about three miles off in the valley. I believe that this route has never been taken before by a European.

I shot a bird here that I had never seen in China before; it was black, with breast and rump of an intense scarlet. During the day I passed coolies carrying tea from Ya-chow-fu to Ta-tsien-lu. This is a shorter but more mountainous road than that usually taken, which makes a larger bend to the southward, but which had been washed away in places lately and rendered impassable, or nearly so.

July 26.—Left Yo-so-po at daylight. The road descends at first and a stream is crossed, a high range has then to be ascended by a very steep and winding road, the sides of the mountains being covered with low scrub. Among the bushes composing it I noticed many species of berberis and a dwarfed holly. At Yang-yung-min the main road is joined again, and at 9.30 A.M. I arrived at Pan-jo, 8,100 feet above the sea. The road continues to ascend until the top of the pass, Tai-hsiang-ling-kwan, 9,270 feet above the sea, is reached. Many asters and primulas were growing and, not far from the top, hydrangeas. The scenery was very fine, and, looking down on the forest which covered the sides of the mountain, some trees could be seen bearing white and pink blossoms, forming a pleasant contrast to the sea of green in which they appeared to be placed. Some of the trees were of large size and there were many species. The whole was a scene of very varied vegetation, and a happy collecting-place for a botanist. Streams of the clearest water rushing down courses on the sides of the mountains, added a freshness to the view. In the evening Huang-ni-po was reached. The roads during the day had been rough, but shady in many places, and just before the halting-place was arrived at, two small suspension bridges were passed over.

July 27.—Arrived at Shih-chia-chiao, a small village seventy li from Ya-chow-fu. The mosquitoes were very troublesome here.

July 28.—Starting at daylight, the road commenced almost immediately to descend. Many coolies were passed, those going westward being loaded with tea in paos or slabs, tobacco, coarse cloth, small china basins, grass sandals, salt, rice and several kinds of paper. Those we overtook going east were carrying iron utensils, probably from Yung-ching-hsien, medicines and coal of apparently good quality. A ridge 3,750 feet above the sea was crossed during the day and Ya-chow-fu reached at 6.30 P.M.

July 29.—This morning I was visited by a custom-house official, who brought a host of underlings with him. His business was to inform me that orders had been received from Cheng-tu directing that I was to travel by Hung-ya-hsien. After changing coolies, dismissing those from Ta-tsien-lu and hiring fresh ones, I found that the loads had to be altered to suit a different system of carrying.

A start was made at 11.30 A.M. and a tributary of the Ya was crossed by myself and a few coolies when a terrific thunderstorm, accompanied by a deluge of rain, caused the river to rise so rapidly that the boat could not return to the other side. I found shelter in a hut that luckily happened to be near. The numerous watercourses filled almost immediately, and poured torrents into the already swollen river. Later in the day the weather cleared, and I pushed on to a village near the Ya River and about fifteen li from Ya-chow-fu. The remainder of the coolies with baggage had been unable to cross, so I was forced to leave them behind. I heard that a sampan had been swamped in the river and that several lives had been lost.

July 30.—The road now led across the river, which was so swollen as to be dangerous to cross, it having rained heavily during the night. At about noon it subsided a little and the passage across was made.

Directly afterwards a heavy rain stopped all progress, as the coolies could not work. Shelter was found in a hut in a small village called Cha-pa built on a steep rocky knoll on the river bank and reached by steps cut in the rock. The banks here are precipitous but vegetation is seen in every possible place on the face of the cliffs.

July 31.—A thick mist in the morning. After travelling fifteen li, the country became hilly and rice was cultivated in terraces. The river had now to be crossed and the passage was dangerous, the current being very strong and with many whirlpools. The river was crossed twice more to-day, and in the evening a halt was made for the night at a village called Tsi-ho-kia.

August 1.—In the morning I discovered that a robbery had taken place during the night, a case containing bird skins having been stolen. This placed me in an awkward position, as the landlord wanted me to remain till he could catch the thief, but I was anxious to report the matter at Hung-ya-hsien and started at 8.30. When the landlord found that I was determined to go, he, with the object of being the first to report, started before me. I had not gone far when one of the Yamen runners came up with the box that had been stolen and which had been found in a field close to the inn. It had been covered with hide at Ta-tsien-lu, and the thief no doubt thought that it contained musk. A small hole had been cut in the lid, and upon the contents being found to be only bird skins, it was thrown away. I was very glad to recover it, for it contained, among others, the skin of a *Lophophorus L'huysii*, and none of them were damaged. After two hours journey the Ya was crossed and Hung-ya-hsien, on the left bank, entered. Here my passport was copied. I found the landlord locked up. When he heard that the stolen property had been recovered he clamoured to be set free, but the authorities would not listen to him. It was not enough they said for the property to be found, the thief must be found before he could be released. When I left he was still in custody, and I have no doubt that before he got his liberty he was squeezed for some thousands of cash.

The innkeepers do not seem to have a very happy time of it, for they are made responsible for robberies committed on their premises, and when officials pass they have to put them up for next to nothing.

Crossing again to the right bank of the Ya I met a French missionary going to Hung-ya-hsien, but in the rapid stream there was no time for anything but a short salute. Arrived at Kia-kiang at 9 P.M.

August 2.—To-day some very fine trees allied to the banyan were passed. I measured one of the largest and found the circumference of the trunk to be 36 ft. I had sent a messenger on ahead to make arrangements for the storage of the collection belonging to Prince Henri till a boat could be hired to take them down the river. On arriving at Kia-ting-fu I went on board my boat and found my collectors suffering from fever and ague brought on by the great heat.

I was also in a very poor state of health, owing to hard work, and the insufficiency and poverty of the food I had been able to obtain, and an attack of dysentery at Ta-tsien-lu had left me in a weak state. Indian-corn cake, rice, and occasionally eggs were the food upon which I had lived for months. Beef and pork were procurable, it is true, at times at Ta-tsien-lu, but the former, being the flesh of worn-out beasts of burden, was so tough as to be uneatable, and as for the pork, no European who has seen the scavenging done by the pigs in towns, would I imagine care to eat it. In the country it is curious to note the difference, for there the pigs are kept very clean and most carefully fed by their owners.

I should mention that my boat was not moored near the city, but about ten li below it, and close to the right bank of the river, on which were growing some remarkably large and graceful clumps of bamboo, which furnished a most welcome shade during the day. The nights were, however, very hot at this season of the year, and sleep difficult to obtain on account of the persecution of a small sand-fly which principally attacked the feet. The bites caused a severe irritation which lasted for about a week.

On August 6 I left at 9.30 A.M. for Omêi-shan, where I hoped to be able to spend several days in more fully exploring the temples than was possible in my previous short visit, and also to see how the collectors had got on with their work. During the day I travelled fifty li, and slept at a small village twenty li from Omêi-hsien. Passing through the latter town on the next day I reached Wan-nien-ssu in the evening, having traversed a highly cultivated valley where much rice is grown. Dotted about were small patches of ground rising slightly above the dead level of the paddy fields, on which clumps of trees were growing, and beneath their shade the farmhouses were built. I found comfortable lodgings in a temple. On August 8 I made an excursion round Wan-nien-ssu, and found that the country had every appearance of being a splendid collecting ground, being very rich in species and covered to a great extent with virgin forest.

One of my coolies who had come from Ta-tsien-lu was here obliged to leave, as he had a bad sore on his back caused by the load he had carried down, and which was part of my botanical collection. I therefore paid him his money, and he went to Kia-ting-fu to get a few things he had left in my boat. After getting them, he was returning to the town in a sampan, when he fell overboard and lost all his hard-earned wages. He was now ten days' journey from home and in a penniless state, but luckily Mr. Kricheldorff had just arrived from Mou-pin, and on applying to him he gave him sufficient cash to enable him to reach his home. This coolie

SUMMIT AND UPPER PART OF PRECIPICE, MOUNT OMÊI.

was a remarkably fine man, standing about 6 ft. 4 in., and was half Tibetan.

On August 9 I left Wan-nien-ssu and continued the ascent of the mountain, the road leading through beautiful scenery, there being many fine forest trees, and in the more open places a luxuriant undergrowth. Some deep gorges are seen, and numerous streams course down the mountain side. Lodging was found in a small temple called Ta-chung-tze. Nearly the whole of the road up the mountain is made of flights of stone steps, and in places they are very steep.

On August 10 the summit was reached at 10 A.M., and here I found Mr. and Mrs. Lewis, of the American Mission, staying at a temple called Chang-fu-ting, or the Thousand Buddha summit. Mrs. Lewis was the first European lady who had ascended the mountain, and she was carried up on the back of a coolie. She told me that this mode of travelling was not at all disagreeable as long as the coolie was moving. When, however, he stopped to rest, and placed the stick under the frame to take the weight off his back, there was a most uncomfortable feeling as if she was on the point of being thrown backwards down the road that had just been ascended. Many Chinese ladies ascend the mountain, and they are all carried up in this way. I remained at the summit for ten days, during most of which time the weather was wet and misty. Occasionally it would clear, and then often clouds could be seen below and to the southward, which, when they struck the face of the precipice, would roll up and envelope the summit in mist. One day only was clear enough to allow the great snowy range of mountains round Ta-tsien-lu to be seen, and at the same time I saw the curiously-terraced shape and flat square summit of Wa-shan to the southward of west.

On two occasions I saw the celebrated Glory of Buddha from the precipice at the 'Golden Summit.' This extraordinary phenomenon is apparently the reflection of the sun upon the upper surface of the clouds beneath, and has the appearance of a golden disc surrounded by radiating bars bearing all the colours of the rainbow. These are constantly moving, and scintillate and change colour in a very remarkable manner.

It is very uncertain when the Glory can be seen, as the sun shining on clouds below does not always produce it, and it may appear at any time when the sun is over a certain height above the horizon. It is held in great respect by the Buddhists, and thousands of pilgrims, some coming from great distances, visit the mountain in the hope of being able to see it. A considerable number of them are so overcome by excess of religious feeling on beholding it, that they throw themselves over the frightful precipice into the clouds upon which it appears, their bodies as a rule falling upon an inaccessible spur covered with forest, perhaps a mile or more below.

There were a good number of pilgrims on the mountain at the time of my visit, but the principal time for pilgrimages is in the autumn, after all the harvest work is completed, which is about the end of September. All the temples are built of wood with tiled roofs, and many have a barnlike appearance, but most of them are fairly rich in idols and incense jars. They have, as a rule, bells, some of great size, and many of them have been damaged by fires, which appear to be very frequent. I saw the ruins of several temples that had been recently destroyed. When a bell has been rendered useless it is thrown outside, and no further care appears to be taken of it. There must be many hundreds of tons of bronze and bell metal laying about uncared for and unsheltered, going to ruin on the mountain. The ruin of the bronze temple at the summit has been mentioned before. No one seems to take the trouble to gather the valuable metal together for recasting or any other purpose. When a temple has been burned, it is nearly always rebuilt, the trees on the mountain being allowed to be used for this purpose and also for the priest's firewood, but for no other purpose; the place, therefore, is not likely to be ever denuded of its timber.

The priests get a good living out of the contributions of the enormous number of pilgrims who visit the mountain. Those living at the summit have, however, a hard time during the winter months, when the temperature is very low, and they are entirely cut off from below for about a month, during which time the road is rendered impassable by snow and ice. No life is allowed to be taken on the mountain, and I nearly got into serious trouble by shooting at a tragopan (*Ceriornis temminki*) which was running across the path, and which I failed to bag. I was well clear of all temples, which occur at intervals of about five li all the way up, but one of my own men must have acted as informer, for on reaching the summit the head priest requested me not to shoot again on the mountain.

Two iron suspension bridges are passed on the way up, but they do not differ in construction from those seen further west.

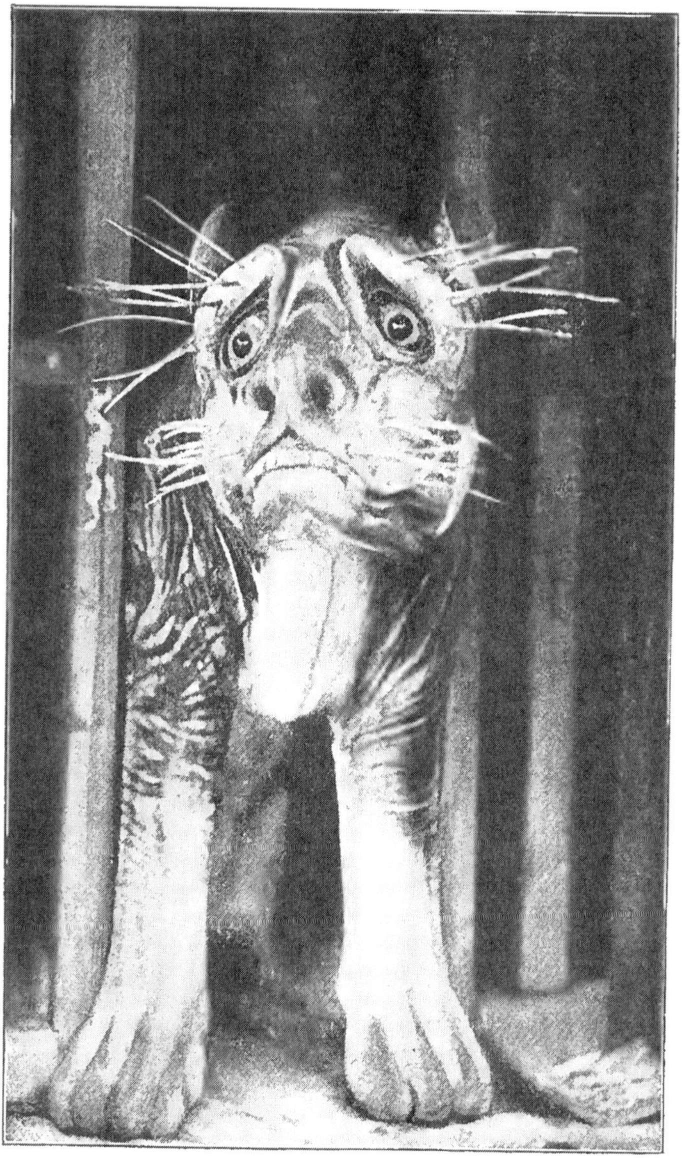

IMAGE OF TIGER NEAR THE SUMMIT OF MOUNT OMÊI.

CHAPTER XV

OMÊI-SHAN TO SHANGHAI AND HOME

Departure from Omêi-shan—Find Mr. Kricheldorff at Kia-ting—His difficulties at Mou-pin—Packing up—Bad conduct of collectors—Flood of Min river—Dangerous position of boat—Expedition to Mantzu caves—New species of bat—Arrival of collectors—Live stock—Leave Kia-ting-fu—Lolo raiders—Leave Sui-fu—Dangerous state of river—Ba-sa-tou—Chung-king—Delayed by state of river—Murders of native converts—Quei-chau collector—Desertion of pilot—Sampan stove in at Hu-lin—Mortality among *Crossoptilon*—Delay at Wu-shan-hsien—Rapid at Niu-kan-tan—Quick travelling—Arrival at Ichang—Sale of boat—Shanghai—The collection of Prince Henri—Leave for Southampton.

On August 17 I left the summit of Omêi-shan on my return to Kia-ting-fu, reaching Su-chi on the evening of the 18th, just at dusk.

Being anxious to reach my boat as soon as possible, I hired two sampans, for myself and my coolies, hoping that with the favouring current the short distance would be quickly and safely traversed.

It soon became very dark, however, and the boatmen seemed to lose either the way or their heads, for before I apprehended any danger, I found that the sampans had been swept into a rapid, and that in the darkness, instead of being kept inshore, had been carried out into the main stream of the Min River, and were in danger of being swept down beyond the place where my boat was anchored. By dint of hard work they were got inshore again, luckily above her, and she was soon found. On getting on board I found Mr. Kricheldorff, who had arrived from Mou-pin on Sunday. He reported having had great difficulty with the natives, who stole his tent and interfered so much with his collectors that he was compelled to abandon the higher and more promising collecting grounds and to take up his residence in a house in the village. The consequence was, that the collection he brought back was anything but what I had expected, and I was much disappointed.

I was now fully employed in arranging and packing the collections already made, hoping to get them out of the way before the collectors I had left behind in Tibet and Ta-tsien-lu should come in with their treasures. A few days after my arrival I received a letter in Chinese from Ta-tsien-lu, complaining of the bad conduct of one of my collectors at Pu-tzu-fong towards a Tibetan girl, and which had so preyed upon her mind that she had hanged herself. Although I greatly deplored the circumstance, for which I was in no way responsible, I was very glad to have left the neighbourhood before it occurred, as I should certainly have got into trouble, and probably have had to pay a heavy indemnity.

On August 24 the river rose rapidly, probably fifteen feet during the day, the boat rocking so much as to prevent writing. This flood was caused by the Tung and Ya Rivers, the Min above the town being in its usual state, so that probably hot weather caused a large quantity of snow to melt in the mountains around Ta-tsien-lu.

The following day the river was still rising, and the boat in an awkward place, from which it was impossible to move her, the river rushing past in a roaring torrent and about twenty-five feet above its ordinary height, being the colour of mud. Three anchors were down, and luckily all the cables held, or we should have been swept miles down the stream and probably wrecked. The water was rushing down the Tung and Ya Rivers with such violence into the Min that it had not time to run down to a level surface, but could be plainly seen running up in the centre to a height of several feet above the level at the banks. Without having seen such a flood it would be difficult to imagine the force of the enormous volume of water so suddenly set free.

On the morning of the 26th the flood began to abate, and as soon as practicable the boat was shifted to a more secure anchorage.

News soon spread about of the disasters caused by the flood, much damage having been done to the crops and villages as well as to the junks and boats. The loss of life also had been, as usual, considerable.

The following day the river continued to fall, though a very heavy rain was falling, and the boat had to be again moved to a safer anchorage.

On August 28 I made a trip to some of the Mantzu caves cut in the red sandstone. These are found on both sides of the river, and those I visited on this occasion were on the right bank, the same side as the town. On attempting to enter one of them I found the mouth so choked with creepers and other plants that they had to be forced aside before I could get in. Inside was a skeleton, but whether of a Chinese or a Mantzu I am unable to say.

The only living inhabitants were bats, of which I captured several, one turning out to be of a species hitherto unknown, and which has now been named *Hipposiderus Prattii*. It has a total length of 5·6 inches, and is coloured dull, smoky grey.

I also obtained at Kia-ting-fu an interesting species of salamander.

On August 30 the mail arrived from Ta-tsien-lu, and I received a letter from Mgr. Biet telling me, among other things, that the full power of government of the town and district had been turned over to the civil mandarin. This will probably be a bad thing for the missionaries, for he is an ignorant man and much prejudiced against foreigners. I took his photograph while there, as he was particularly anxious to have it done.

My collectors arrived the next day, having been delayed slightly on their journey down by the floods on the Ya River. They had all done very well, and I got the collections on board at once to arrange and pack. The living specimens consisted of fifty-three *Crossoptilon* (mentioned before), three Amherst pheasants, one *Lophophorus L'huysii*, two pheasants (*Phasianus decollatus*), one tragopan and two bear cubs. There was no room in my boat for these, and I was obliged to hire a large sampan for their conveyance. I also got the French missionaries to hire a boat for the collection I had taken charge of for Prince Henri, as I thought they would be able to do so on more advantageous terms than I could. They only chartered her for the voyage to Chung-king, however, and at that place I had to hire afresh. All my arrangements were completed on September 4. Mr. Vale, of the China Inland Mission, came on board and said good-bye, and a start for home was made at twelve o'clock, with such a strong current in our favour that Sui-fu was reached the next day.

Here Messrs. Wellwood and Warner, both missionaries, came on board to see me. We overtook at this place two hundred soldiers who had passed down the Min River from Cheng-tu a few days previously, and were on their way to Lolo-ping, at which place there had been a Lolo raid, further disturbances being expected, as the Lolos, according to their invariable custom, had given notice that they intended to make further plundering excursions into the Chinese territory.

Leaving Sui-fu on September 6, I found the Yangtze still very high, this being too early in the season for it to run low. Several dangerous places were encountered during the day, but all were passed in safety.

The strength of the current here at this time of the year would render it impossible, in my opinion, for any steamer to get up against it, unless of exceptional power and speed. The reefs also are very dangerous, often running out into the river just where a sharp bend occurs, requiring a very handy vessel and great skill in management to avoid disaster. The Chinese pilots are very clever in navigating the native boats through such places, but still, accidents are frequent.

On the night of the 7th, the boat was secured off the town of Ba-sa-tou, celebrated for its distilleries, where native spirit, known as samshew, is produced in large quantities. Here I saw the last of the long, narrow bamboo rafts which were familiar sights further up the river. They appear to be extensively used for the transport of the spirit, the jars containing it being stowed in a single row for nearly the whole length.

I landed, but the conduct of the natives rendered it prudent for me to return on board as soon as possible.

Chung-king is 230 li further down, and was reached at 2 P.M. the following day without anything occurring worthy of notice, except that one of the large huloes broke when the boat was in a dangerous place. Luckily no accident occurred, but there was no spare one on board as there always should be.

I found Mr. Cockburn, the British Resident, still here, his successor, Mr. Fulford, having been wrecked on his passage up, and being now forced to return to Hankow and wait for the river to fall.

Owing to the high, changeable and dangerous state of the river—it rose fifteen feet in one day during my enforced stay—I was not able to leave for some days, and while thus delayed, I was most kindly entertained, as on former occasions, by Mr. Cockburn, and I had also the pleasure of the society of several Europeans, Mr. and Mrs. Wilson, English missionaries, and Dr. and Mrs. Cameron. The Doctor had, some years ago, made a journey to Bhamo unaccompanied by any other European. While I was here, two French missionaries came in from Ta-tsu, said to be 200 li distant, and from which place they had, with difficulty, escaped with their lives, a reward of 200 taels having been offered for their heads. A few days later the news came from Ta-tsu of the cruel murder of eleven native converts, who were reported to have been some boiled and others burnt to death by the savage mob. All the mission-houses and property having been looted and then destroyed.

The collector I had despatched, when on my way up the river, to Quei-chau, returned here just before I did, having received orders to be here in August. He had made a very good collection of lepidoptera, and had some long series of interesting cicadas. I should imagine that this poor province would be a very good field for a naturalist. It is known to abound in minerals.

On September 18, the river had fallen so much as to be considered safe for boats, and all was got ready to start. Just before leaving I was disagreeably surprised to find the pilot missing, and soon found that he had deserted, taking with him part of his wages in advance, which, according to general practice, I had paid him. The engagement of another caused some delay, and after saying good-bye to all my kind friends at Chung-king, we left at 2 P.M.

The river being so high and the current so strong, rapid progress was made. The night after leaving it fell 2½ feet, as I measured on a stick stuck in the bottom, close to the boat, for the purpose. This, however, made but little difference in the rapidity of the stream, and whirlpools and strong eddies were very frequent. Though many dangerous places were passed, no damage was done until Hu-lin was reached. Just below this place the sampan containing all my living specimens, struck hard upon a rock and knocked a hole in her bottom. This was temporarily stopped in the usual way, by ramming in a handful of rags, a supply of which always appears to be kept handy for such purpose in navigating this river. She then came on and caught us up at our evening anchorage, her crew being anxious to reach us before making any further repairs as my boat carried all the food. She now had to be completely unloaded, baled out, and then have the damage made good in the best way that we could manage it. This did not take much time, and she was loaded again the same night and remained fairly watertight till I had finished with her at Ichang.

The *Crossoptilon* were by this time much reduced in numbers, many having died from want of strength to stand the voyage, all being under six months old. The other birds, being mature, stood the journey much better.

A slight delay occurred at Wu-shan-hsien, where we were forced to remain a day, the whirlpools and current in the Wu-shan Gorge being reported as too dangerous for my boats to pass through. The river, however, fell during the day and night, and we were able to proceed, but found the stream in the gorge still very violent. The wrecks of two junks were passed in it, the crews being busy saving what they could from them.

At Niu-kan-tan, the worst rapid in the river, when it is at this height, was passed, the boat being tossed about like a cork among the immense whirlpools. Below it, many junks were waiting for the river to fall, the ascent being now impossible. The Sin-tan and Ta-tung rapids I found to be perfectly smooth but the current very strong, the river being fifteen feet higher than when I passed down last year.

Ichang was reached on September 25, the journey down the river from Chung-king, a distance of four hundred miles, having been made in fifty hours and forty-five minutes, as will be seen by the time-table below, the journey up having taken twenty-two days.

Date		Time under way H	M
September	18	3	0
,,	19	7	10
,,	20	3	30
,,	21	11	30
,,	22	9	25
,,	23	3	0
,,	24	9	30
,,	25	3	40
		50	45

I was now fully engaged in arranging and repacking the collections, paying my men off finally, and giving them the usual cumshaw, which, of course, varied in amount according to the time they had been with me, and the way in which they had behaved.

I was lucky enough to find an immediate purchaser for my boat, which I had feared might wait a long time on my hands, such articles not being in frequent demand at Ichang. She had been well looked after, however, and in spite of her four journeys up and down the river was as good as new.

Waiting here for the river to fall, in order to get to Chung-king, were Mr. Hobson, Commissioner of Customs, with his staff, and Mr. Fulford, Consul, who were going there to open the port to European trade. No steamers belonging to foreigners were, however, to be allowed to proceed above this port.

When all my work was completed, I took a passage in the steamer *Kiang-yung*, which carried me to Shanghai without the nuisance of changing boats at Hankow. On my arrival I had a bad attack of fever, which I felt more severely through being in a weak state of health, I having for the last year, nearly, subsisted almost entirely upon the poor food consumed by the lower classes of Chinese.

While here, Mr. T. Wood, whom I had previously met

at Hankow, kindly gave me the use of his godown for the rearrangement and packing of my collection. In it I had ample room to spread everything out, and could ascertain exactly the size and number of tin-lined cases that would be required for their transport to England. I found that by an oversight all my reptilia had been left behind at Ichang, but upon sending a message I had a reply to say that they were all safe and would be forwarded. They reached England safely, shortly after I did.

I had also to relieve myself of the responsibility of the care of the collection belonging to Prince Henri of Orleans, which was still on board the steamer. My instructions were to leave it with the French Consul at Hankow, but when I passed that place the consul was away. I therefore took it on to Shanghai, intending to turn it over to the consul there, but upon my calling upon him, he refused to have anything to do with it, excusing himself by saying that the care of such valuable articles was too great a responsibility. In consequence of this refusal, I was obliged to leave it with the French missionaries, who arranged for its shipment to Europe.

During my stay in Shanghai I found most comfortable quarters in the splendid club, of which, through the courtesy of the members, I was a temporary member.

On October 22 I left in the S.S. *Neckar* for Southampton, at which port I arrived on December 4. To my great disappointment, my Tibetan dog, Ja-ma, died in the Mediterranean. When I showed him to the genial captain of the *Neckar* he utterly refused to have him on board unless caged, and this I was obliged to have done. He was certainly the largest dog I have ever seen, and handsome as well. Though he had bitten severely several Chinese, I never knew him attack a European.

One of the bears also died on the passage, the other being sent to the Zoological Gardens.

I had originally intended to supplement this book with an appendix, giving the names of all the new species obtained during my journey, but in the case of the lepidoptera this has been found to be impracticable, as the classification is likely to extend over several years. The few only that have as yet been named are given.

I have to thank Dr. A Günther for his valuable remarks upon my collection of reptilia and fish.

I cannot conclude without expressing great regret at the way in which the missionaries, from whom I received much valuable assistance, have lately been treated, but several incidents that I have mentioned will show what a credulous and cowardly race the Chinese are.

TCHONG-TSAO (*Sphæria sinensis*)

APPENDICES

I.

List of Birds collected in China by Mr. A. E. Pratt

Pica pica.
Garrulus sinensis.
Cryptolopha affinis.
Merula Kessleri.
,, ruficollis.
Myiophoneus cæruleus.
Ruticilla auroræa.
Phylloscopus occipitalis.
,, superciliosus.
Cinclus Pallasi.
Spizixus semitorques.
Pycnonotus xanthorrhous.
Trochalopterum canorum.
,, Ellioti.
Dryonastes perspicillatus.
,, sannio.
Henicurus sinensis.
Microcichla Scouleri.
Yulima diademata.
Suthora suffusa.
Grandala cælicolor.
Niltava sundara.
Pyrrhocorax graculus.
Corvus pastinator.
Parus Beavani.
,, minor.
,, venustulus.
,, monticolus.
Acridula glaucogularis.
,, concinna.
Troglodytes nipalensis.
Tichodroma muraria.
Lanius erythronotus.
,, Schacti.
Cotile riparia.
Anthus Blakistoni.
Motacilla leucopsis.
,, flava.
Emberiza castaneiceps.
,, pusilla.
,, elegans.
Eophona melanura.
Poliopsar cineraceus.
Cuculus canorus.
Gecinus Guerini.
Pericrocotus brevirostris.
Pomatorhinus gravivox.
Trochalopteron Ellioti.

Leucodiopteron chinense.
Coccothraustes carneiceps.
Carpodacus dubius.
„ rubicilloides.
Æthopyga Dabryi.
Picus Cabanisi.
„ mandarinus.
Picoides funebris.
Iyngipicus scintilliceps.
Ardea prasinosceles.
Ibidorhynchus Struthersi.
Scolopax rusticula.
„ solitaria.
Gallicrex cristatus.
Crossoptilon Tibetanum.
Ceriornis temminki.
Lophophorus L'huysii.
Pucrasia xanthospila.
Thaumalea Amherstiæ.
„ picta.
Phasianus decollatus.
Lerwa nivicola.
Ithaginis Geoffroyi.
Vanellus cristatus.
Ægialites placidus.
Himantopus candidus.
Querquedula falcata.
Podiceps philippensis.

LOPHOPHORUS L'HUYSII

CROSSOPTILON TIBETANUM

II

List of the Species of Reptiles and Fishes collected by Mr. A. E. Pratt on the Upper Yang-tze-kiang and in the province Sze-chuen, with description of the New Species. By Albert Günther, M.A., M.D., Ph.D., F.R.S.

THE following notes contain, besides the species described in the 'Annals and Magazine of Natural History,' 1888, vol. I., and 1889, vol. IV., all those contained in the last collections brought home by Mr. Pratt.

TORTOISES

1. *Emys reevesii* (Gray). Mountains north of the Kiu-kiang.

The ornamental colours of the soft parts are distributed as follows:—They consist of yellow bands and spots, edged with black; the most conspicuous is a band running from the upper part of the eye along the upper margin of the neck; sometimes it is interrupted in some part of its course, and generally a continuation of it is visible in front of the eye. A short curved band between the eye and the tympanum, another running from the lower part of the eye to below the tympanum; an oblong spot at the posterior angle of the mandible. Tympanum and post-tympanic region with curved streaks and spots. Sides and lower part of the neck with parallel straight bands, posteriorly broken up into series of spots. In very young examples these ornamentations are less numerous.

2. *Trionyx sinensis* (Wiegm.). Vicinity of Kiu-kiang.

LIZARDS

3. *Tachydromus septentrionalis* (Gthr.). Common in the mountains north of Kiu-kiang.

4. *Tachydromus wolteri* (Fisch.). Much scarcer.

5. *Lygosoma reevesii* (Gray). Mountains north of Kiu-kiang, and at Mo-si-mien Pass in the province of Sze-chuen (alt. 12,800 ft.).

6. *Lygosoma elegans* (Blgr.). One specimen from the mountains north of Kiu-kiang.

7. *Eumeces xanthi*, sp. n.

This species is of special interest inasmuch as it is most closely allied to the Californian *Eumeces skiltonianus*, from which it is barely distinguishable by a somewhat different coloration and by the postfrontals being widely separate from each other, whilst they are more or less in contact in the American form.

Snout of moderate length. Nasal small, followed by a postnasal, which forms a suture with the first two labials; anterior loreal forming a suture with the frontonasal; four supraoculars, the three anterior in contact with the vertical; occipitals entirely separated by the central occipital; two pairs of nuchals; seventh upper labial largest; two or three very obtuse tubercles on the anterior border of the ear, which is smaller than a dorsal scale; two azygos postmentals. Twenty-four or twenty-six scales round the body, the dorsal much broader than the lateral and ventral. Limbs overlapping when pressed against the body; the length of the hind limb is contained twice and a half to twice and two-thirds in the distance from snout to vent. A median series of transversely enlarged subcaudals. Dark olive above, with a black lateral band extending from the loreal region to the tail; the band is bordered above and below by a light streak, which again has a blackish margin. Four series of dorsal scales separate the two lateral bands. Sometimes a light longitudinal band edged with black runs along the median line of the back and of the tail. Belly greenish blue.

Four specimens were collected by Mr. Pratt at Ichang, of which the largest is 6½ inches long, the trunk and head measuring 2¾ inches.

8. *Japalura yunnanensis* (Anders.). Ichang.

9. *Gecko japonicus* (D. and B.). Mountains north of Kiu-kiang.

10. *Calamaria quadrimaculata* (D. & B.). Mountains north of Kiu-kiang.

11. *Simotes chinensis*, sp. n.

Scales in seventeen rows. Eight upper labials, the fourth and fifth entering the orbit; loreal square; one præ- and two postoculars; anterior chin-shields in contact with four lower labials. Ventral shields 190, distinctly keeled on the sides; subcaudals 63, anal entire. The ground-colour is a light brownish grey; trunk crossed by thirteen, tail by four narrow, equidistant, black cross-bars; these are somewhat broader on the back than on the sides, and indistinctly edged with white. A black band from eye to eye and côntinued over the fifth and sixth labials. The black, arrow-shaped spot on the neck is well-defined. Abdomen with numerous square black spots, each occupying one-half or the whole of a ventral scute. Subcaudals uniform white.

One young specimen measures 8½ inches, the tail being 2 inches long.

12. *Achalinus rufescens* (Blgr.). One specimen, uniformly black, from Ichang.

13. *Ablabes chinensis*, sp. n.

This species belongs to that group of the genus of which *Ablabes melanocephalus* is the type; it comes nearest to *Ablabes humberti*, having, like that species, ten upper labial shields, the eighth of which is excluded from the labial margin. But it differs by having a longer tail and by its less ornamented coloration.

Scales in seventeen rows. One præocular, two postoculars. The occipital does not touch the lower postocular; temporals 1 + 2, the anterior in contact with both postoculars. Ventrals 182; of the tail nearly one-half has been lost, the mutilated part being protected by fifty-three pairs of subcaudals, so that the whole number may be estimated to have been between eighty and ninety. Upper parts nearly uniform brownish grey, the posterior part of the trunk indistinctly showing a series of whitish spots along each side of the back. No black dots along the vertebral line. The black cross bands between the eyes and on the neck are present as in *Ablabes humberti* and *Ablabes collaris*, but much less distinct. Abdomen white, each ventral shield with a black dot on each side.

One specimen was found by Mr. Pratt at Ichang; its trunk measures fifteen inches, and its tail was probably 5½ inches in length.

14. *Coluber rufo-dorsatus* (Cant.). Common in the vicinity of Kiu-kiang.

15. *Elaphis dione* (Pall.). Vicinity of Kiu-kiang.

16. *Elaphis sauromates* (Pall.). Common near Kiu-kiang. Mr. Boulenger has discovered that *Phyllophis carinata* (Gthr.) is the young of this species.

17. *Zaocys dhumnades* (Cant.). Common near Kiu-kiang.

18. *Ptyas korros* (Reinw). One specimen from Kiu-kiang.

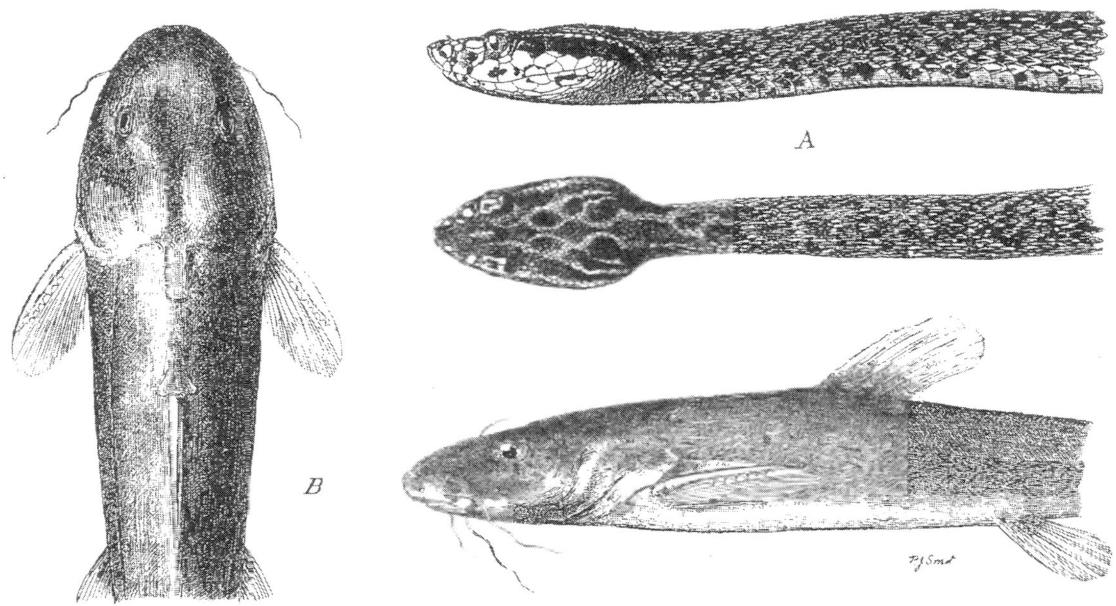

PLATE 1.

19. *Cyclophis major* (Gthr.). Common near Kiu-kiang.

20. *Tropidonotus annularis* (Hallow.). Common near Kiu-kiang.

21. *Tropidonotus tigrinus* (Boie). Very common near Kiu-kiang.

22. *Tropidonotus swinhonis* (Gthr.). Ichang.

23. *Tropidonotus macrophthalmus* (Gthr.). Kia-tiang-fu in Sze Chuen (alt. 1,070 ft.).

24. *Ophites septentrionalis* (Gthr.). One specimen from the neighbourhood of Kiu-kiang.

25. *Lycodon rufozonatus* (Cant.). Common at Kiu-kiang and at Kia-tiang-fu, Sze Chuen.

26. *Bungarus semifasciatus* (Kuhl). One specimen from the country near Kiu-kiang.

27. *Callophis annularis* (Gthr.). One specimen from the country near Kiu-kiang.

28. *Trimeresurus xanthomelas*, sp. n. (Plate I. Fig. A.)

The second upper labial shield forms the front part of the facial pit; upper part of the snout with three small shields in front. Supraciliary scute large, not divided. Scales in twenty-one rows, keeled. Ventrals 185, 189; subcaudals 59, 68: anal and præanal not divided. Black, each scale with an elongate greenish-yellow spot, the spot frequently including small black specks. By the modification of the extent of the black colour on the scales a chain of subrhombic spots is formed along the vertebral line; the yellow of the scales within each rhombic spot is of a more reddish shade. Upper part of the head black, with a pattern of narrow symmetrical lines; a deep black band from the eye to the angle of the mouth; labial shields yellow, with a series of black spots on the sutures. A rather indistinct row of black spots along the sides of the body. Lower parts yellow, marbled with black, the black colour predominating in the posterior half of the length.

Five specimens of this beautiful snake were obtained at Ichang by Mr. Pratt, one of the largest being thirty-one inches long, the tail measuring five inches. Mr. Boulenger considers it to be identical with *T. jerdonii* (Gthr.) from the Khassya Hills, but by its striking coloration it forms at any rate a well-marked variety. It feeds on mice; and the specimen I extracted from its stomach proved to be an undescribed species.

29. *Trimeresurus monticola* (Gthr.). Kia-tiang-fu in the province of Sze Chuen (alt. 1,070 ft.).

30. *Halys blomhoffii* (Boie). Common near Kiu-kiang.

31. *Halys acutus*, sp. n.

This new species may be at once recognised by the upper part of the extremity of the snout being produced into a short, flexible, pointed lobe which projects from between the anterior frontal and the rostral shield The anterior frontals are small, longer than broad; the posterior very large, intermediate in size between the anterior frontals and the occipitals. Eye surrounded by a ring of small orbitals, of which those in front are rather elongate ; that below the eye is likewise long and crescent-shaped, separated by a small postocular from the superciliary shield. Seven upper labials, of which the second forms the anterior wall of the antorbital pit, the third and fourth being the largest. A series of three large temporal shields occupies the lower part of the temple, the space between this series and the occipital being covered by ordinary scales.

Scales strongly keeled, the keels forming a high sharp ridge on the posterior part of the body. Each scale bears, besides the keel, on its extremity a pair of very small nodules; scales in twenty-one rows. Ventral shields 160; anal entire; subcaudals 60, of which the six or twenty anterior may be single. Extremity of the tail compressed, covered with comparatively large vertical scutes, and terminating in a long and compressed spine.

The colour of the upper parts is brown, each side of the body being ornamented with a series of large dark-coloured triangles, the point of each triangle meeting that of the other side in the median line of the back. Lower parts whitish with a series of large rounded black spots on each side and smaller ones of irregular shape in the middle. The upper part of the head is uniform black ; a sharp line, which runs from the eye along the middle of the temporal scutes to the angle of the mouth, divides the black coloration of the upper parts from the white of the lower.

This species is very remarkable, not only on account of the rostral lobe, but also for the modification of the scutellation of its compressed tail. Although this modification cannot in any way be taken as an initial step in the development of the rattle of *Crotalus*, the rattle being a modification of the last dermal scute only into which the vertebral column is not prolonged, yet the tail of this species may exercise in a much smaller degree the same function as in the rattlesnake, and may be an instrument by which vibrations and sound are produced. It is well known also that many innocuous snakes are able to vibrate the extremity of their tail. To judge from its size and from the development of its poisonous apparatus this snake must be extremely dangerous.

Three specimens are in the collection, of which the largest is forty-six inches long, the tail measuring 6½ inches. It has been figured in *Ann. Mag. Nat. Hist.* 1888, I. pl. 12.

BATRACHIANS

1. *Rana boulengeri*, sp. n.

This species belongs to that division of the genus of which *Rana kuhlii* and *Rana liebigii* are characteristic forms.

Vomerine teeth in two short oblique series, each starting from the inner edge of the choana. Head large, broad, much depressed; snout very short and rounded; canthus rostralis short but distinct; upper eyelid a little broader than the interorbital space; tympanum hidden. First finger longer than the second; toes with swollen extremity, entirely webbed; subarticular tubercles well developed; inner metatarsal tubercle elongate; no outer tubercle. The tibio-tarsal joint does not reach the end of the snout when the limb is carried forward. Skin of the upper parts covered with large elongate warts and small rounded tubercles; a strong fold of the skin above the tympanum; no glandular fold on the side of the back. Uniform blackish brown above. Male with two internal vocal sacs.

As in *Rana liebigii*, the breeding male has extremely thick forearms, but without any special armature. The rudimentary thumb and the large rounded tubercle on the upper side of the first finger are thickly studded with horny spines, the second and third fingers having similar spines, but less numerous. The whole of the chest is covered with smaller and larger rounded tubercles, each armed with a black conical horny spine, and similar but smaller dermal structures are scattered over the abdomen and also over the throat.

Two specimens of this large species were sent by Mr. Pratt from Ichang. The length from the snout to the vent is four inches.

2. *Bufo vulgaris*. At Ichang and at Kia-tiang-fu (alt. 1,070 ft.).

3. *Megalobatrachus maximus*. One specimen from Kia-tiang-fu (alt. 1,070 ft.).

4. *Hynobius chinensis*, sp. n.

Allied to the Japanese *Hynobius nebulosus*, but with the series of vomerine teeth much shorter, extending backwards only to the middle of the eye-ball. General habit short and stout; head large, nearly as broad as long, its length being rather more than one-fourth of the length of the trunk. Tail compressed in its whole length, but without crest; body with eleven lateral folds. The limbs meet when adpressed; fifth toe well developed; no carpal or tarsal tubercles. Skin smooth; gular fold indistinct. Nearly uniform horny black, the lower parts brownish, finely marbled with darker.

Total length	85 millim
From snout to cloaca	46 „
Length of head	11 „
Width of head	10 „
Fore limb	15 „
Hind limb	16 „
Tail	39 „

Two specimens were collected by Mr. Pratt at Ichang.

FISHES

1. *Acipenser dabryanus* (Dum.). Ichang.

2. *Acipenser*, sp. inc., young specimens from Kiu-kiang.

3. *Psephurus gladius* (Martens). Kiu-kiang.

4. *Eleotris xanthi*, sp. n. D. 6/⅛. A. 1/7. L. lat. 33.

Præoperculum without spine. Twelve series of scales between the origin of the second dorsal fin and the anal. The scales on the neck, cheek, and opercles are small and do not extend on to the interorbital space. Scales finely ciliated. The height of the body is one-fourth of the total length (without caudal); the length of the head two-sevenths. Eye rather small, shorter than the snout, one-fifth of the length of the head, and exceeding the width of the interorbital space. Head rather compressed and high behind, with broad snout, and the lower jaw prominent. The maxillary extends to the vertical from the front margin of the orbit. Gill-membranes attached to the median line of the isthmus. Vertical fins lower than the body; caudal fin rounded, equal in length to the pectorals, which are three-fifths of the length of the head. Light-coloured, with broad, indistinct, darker cross bands on the sides. Dorsal and caudal fins indistinctly spotted with brown; no spot at the base of the pectoral fin.

This species, of which there is only one specimen in the collection, 2½ inches long, is allied to *Eleotris potamophila*, but readily distinguished from it by its narrow, scaleless, interorbital space. I do not know of any other species of this genus ascending in fresh water to a similar distance from the sea.

5. *Ophiocephalus argus* (Cant.). Kiu-kiang.

6. *Polyacanthus opercularis* (L.). Kiu-kiang.

7. *Mastacembelus chinensis* (Blkr.). Ichang.

8. *Silurus asotus* (L.). Kiu-kiang and Kia-tiang-fu.

9. *Macrones longirostris* (Gthr.). Kiu-kiang.

10. *Macrones macropterus* (Blkr.). Kia-tiang-fu and Kiu-kiang.

11. *Macrones crassilabris* (Gthr.). Kiu-kiang and Kia-tiang-fu.

12. *Macrones tæniatus* (Gthr.). Kiu-kiang.

13. *Macrones vachellii* (Rich.). Kiu-kiang.

14. *Macrones pratti*, sp. n. D. 1/6. A. 19. (Plate I. Fig. B.)

Head smooth above, covered with a thin skin; also the bones on the nape are covered with skin. Occipital process narrow, about four times as long as broad; basal bone of the dorsal spine elongate, triangular, nearly as long as the occipital process, from which it is separated by an interspace. Body much elongate, its depth being one-ninth of the total length without caudal, the length of the head nearly one-fifth. Snout broad, obtusely rounded, twice and a half as long as the eye, which is one-seventh of the length of the head. Mouth inferior, as wide as the snout. Teeth on the palate in an uninterrupted concentric band, which is narrower than that of the inter-maxillaries. Barbels very thin, the nasal filaments extending not beyond, and those of the maxillaries somewhat behind, the orbit. Dorsal spine not serrated, lower than the body; pectoral spine a little longer, stronger, strongly denticulated interiorly. Adipose fin about as long as anal. Caudal notched. Coloration nearly uniform.

One specimen 8¼ inches long. Kia-tiang-fu, 1,070 feet, province Sze Chuen.

M. Sauvage describes in *Ann. Sc. Nat.* 1874, i. p. 7, a *Liocassis torosilabris* which I thought might be our species, but the latter has neither movable labial teeth nor a denticulated dorsal spine longer than the pectoral.

15. *Glyptosternum conirostrum* (Steind.). Mountain streams running into the Min River, Sze Chuen.

16. *Exostoma davidi* = *Chimarrhichthys davidi* (Sauvage). From the same locality.

17. *Amblyceps marginatus*, sp. n. D. 1/6. A. 15. P. 1/7. V. 6. (Plate II. Fig. A.)

Head very broad and depressed, but little longer than wide; its length is one-fourth of the total (without caudal); the greatest depth of the body is nearly one-sixth of the same length. Eyes very small, almost immediately behind the upper lip. Barbels well developed, the maxillary and the outer one of the mandible are the longest, reaching to the middle of the pectoral fin, the nasal and the inner one of the mandible only half as long. Mouth wide, anterior, with the lower jaw a little longer than the upper. The maxillary band of teeth is about three times as wide as long. Fins enveloped at the base in thick skin. Dorsal fin with the first ray osseous, its origin being midway between the end of the snout and the adipose fin. Adipose fin low and long, about as long as the anal fin. Pectoral fin, with the first ray long and serrated, extending backwards to below the middle of the dorsal. Ventral fins at some distance behind the dorsal, short, not extending to the anal. Caudal subtruncated.

Brownish-black with broad pure white margins to all the fins.

Length 4½ inches. From mountain streams running into the Min River, province Sze Chuen.

18. *Carassius auratus* (L.). Kiu-kiang.

19. *Pseudogobio sinensis* (Kner). Kiu-kiang.

20. *Pseudogobio productus* (Ptrs.). Kiu-kiang.

21. *Pseudogobio maculatus* sp. n. D. 10. A. 8. L. lat. 41. L. transv. 4/5.

Barbels none. Body rather compressed, its greatest depth being equal to the length of the head and one-fourth of the total (without caudal); snout rather compressed, of moderate length, a little longer than the eye, the diameter of which is nearly one-fourth of the length of the head. Interorbital space convex, as wide as the orbit. Mouth very small, sub-anterior; lower lip interrupted in the middle. The origin of the dorsal fin is nearer to the end of the snout than to the root of the caudal; ventrals inserted below the middle of the dorsal; caudal fin moderately forked; pectoral not quite so long as the head, extending to the origin of the dorsal fin, but not to the root of the ventral. Silvery, with large, irregular, deep black spots, each occupying one or more scales; anterior part of the dorsal fin and a band along each caudal lobe black.

Two specimens, the larger of which is three inches long, are in the collection.

This species would belong, on account of the absence of barbels, to Bleeker's genus *Sarcochilichthys*.

22. *Rhinogobio cylindricus*, sp. n. D. 11. A. 8. L. lat. 48. L. transv. 6/7.

Body low, subcylindrical, its greatest depth being contained five-and-a-half times in the total length (without caudal), the length of the head four times and a fourth. Head low, with the snout much elongate and pointed, the eye being rather nearer to the gill-opening than to the end of the snout; the projecting part of the snout is swollen, conical, the mouth being entirely at the lower side of the snout. Eye one-fifth of the

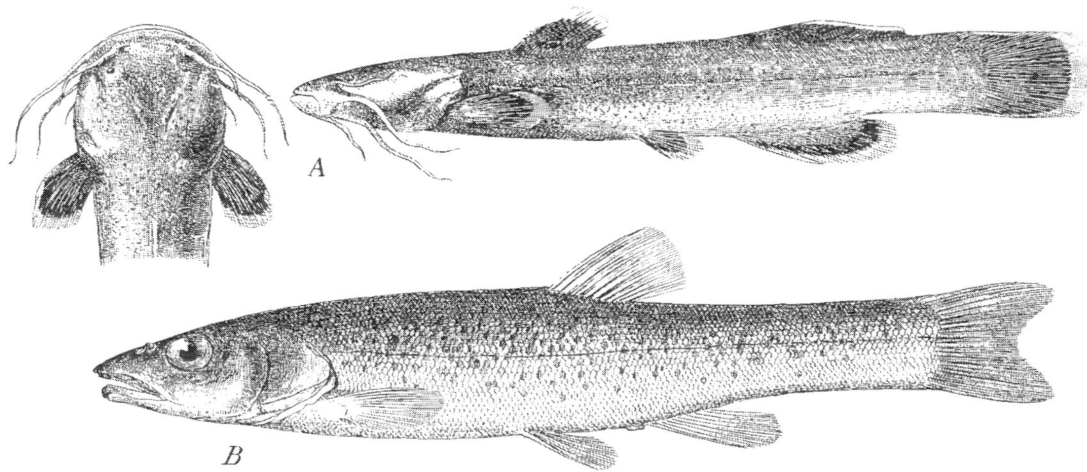

PLATE II.

length of the head, less wide than the flat interorbital space. Upper lip swollen; lower very short, broadly interrupted in the middle; barbel very short, lying in a groove which extends forward to near the extremity of the snout. Gill-membrane attached to the side of the isthmus. The origin of the dorsal fin is considerably nearer to the end of the snout than to the root of the caudal; ventrals inserted below the posterior half of the dorsal. Caudal deeply forked. The pectorals are much shorter than the head, and scarcely extend to the origin of the dorsal fin. The lower parts of the head and of the thoracic region entirely scaleless. Coloration transparent, without any spots.

One specimen, 4 inches long.

This species differs from *Rhinogobio typus* in having a much smaller eye and in having the lower parts of the thorax scaleless.

23. *Barbus sarana* (H. B.) Kia-tiang-fu.

24. *Rhynchocypris variegata*, g. et sp. n. D. 10 or 11. A. 9. L. lat. 100. (Plate II. Fig. B. Two views of the head are also shown at the bottom of Plate III.)

Body rather elongate, its height being two-ninths of the total length (without caudal), the length of the head two-sevenths. Head depressed, broad and flat above; snout wedge-shaped and produced. Eye of moderate size, two-ninths of the length of the head and two-thirds of the length of the snout or of the width of the interorbital space. Origin of the dorsal fin nearer to the root of the caudal than to the extremity of the snout; the anal fin commences at a short distance behind the dorsal and terminates a long way from the caudal; caudal fin emarginate. All the fins are short rayed; the pectorals are not much longer than half the length of the head and terminate at a considerable distance from the ventrals. The root of the ventrals occupies nearly the middle between the end of the snout and the root of the caudal fin; they nearly reach the vent. Lateral line complete, well developed, running along the middle of the body. Back greyish, sides and lower parts silvery; numerous scales on the sides blackish.

This small species grows to a length of five inches. Several specimens were collected by Mr. Styan in mountain streams near Kiu-kiang, and others at Ichang by Mr. Pratt.

25. *Pseudorasbora parva* (Schleg.). Kiu-kiang.

26. *Xenocypris argentea* (Gthr.) Kiu-kiang.

27. *Ctenopharyngodon idellus* (C. V.). Kiu-kiang.

28. *Rhodeus sinensis* (Gthr.). Kiu-kiang and Kia-tiang-fu.

29. *Ochetobius elongatus* (Kner). Kiu-kiang.

30. *Squaliobarbus curriculus* (Rich.). Kiu-kiang.

31. *Hypophthalmichthys molitrix* (C. V.) Kiu-kiang.

32. *Chanodichthys pekinensis* (Basil). Kiu-kiang.

33. *Culter ilishæformis* (Blkr.). Kiu-kiang.

34. *Hemiculter leuciscuius* (Kner). Kiu-kiang.

35. *Luciobrama typus* (Blkr). Kiu-kiang.

36. *Homaloptera fimbriata*, sp. n. D. 11. A. 7. P. 19. V. 11. (Plate III. Fig. A.)

This species differs from the typical species of *Homaloptera* in the shape of its snout and in the arrangement of the barbels. The snout is flat and spatulate, considerably narrowed in front and nearly as long as broad; the mouth is surrounded with fringes, from which the barbels differ only by their greater size; the barbels and fringes of the upper jaw arranged in two concentric series, two pairs of barbels standing in the outer series; behind each angle of the mouth there is a third pair of barbels.

Scales minute and smooth, but there are a few larger ones along the median line of the back and along the lateral line. Origin of the anal fin rather nearer to the root of the caudal than to the occiput. Eyes very small, much nearer to the gill-opening than to the end of the snout; ventral fins opposite to the anterior half of the dorsal. Pectoral fins not extending to the ventrals. Body with broad, indistinct, dark cross bands; pectoral, ventral, and caudal fins with greyish spots.

Three specimens, 4½ inches long, from Ichang and the Min River.

37. *Homaloptera abbreviata*, sp. n. D. 11. A. 7. P. 23. V. 14–15. L. lat. 75. (Plate III. Fig. B.)

The scales are smooth and very small; those of the lateral line are somewhat larger, and seventy-five perforated scales can be counted in it. Snout rounded and nearly twice as long as the postorbital part of the head. Barbels short and simple; upper lip fringed, but not the lower. The dorsal fin occupies the middle between the snout and caudal fin, its origin being somewhat behind that of the ventrals. Pectorals extending beyond the origin of the ventrals; caudal deeply forked.

Upper parts dark coloured, fins yellowish, lower caudal lobe with a diffuse, blackish longitudinal band.

One specimen four inches long from mountain streams running into the Min River, Province Sze Chuen.

38. *Misgurnus anguillicaudatus* (Cant.). Kiu-kiang.

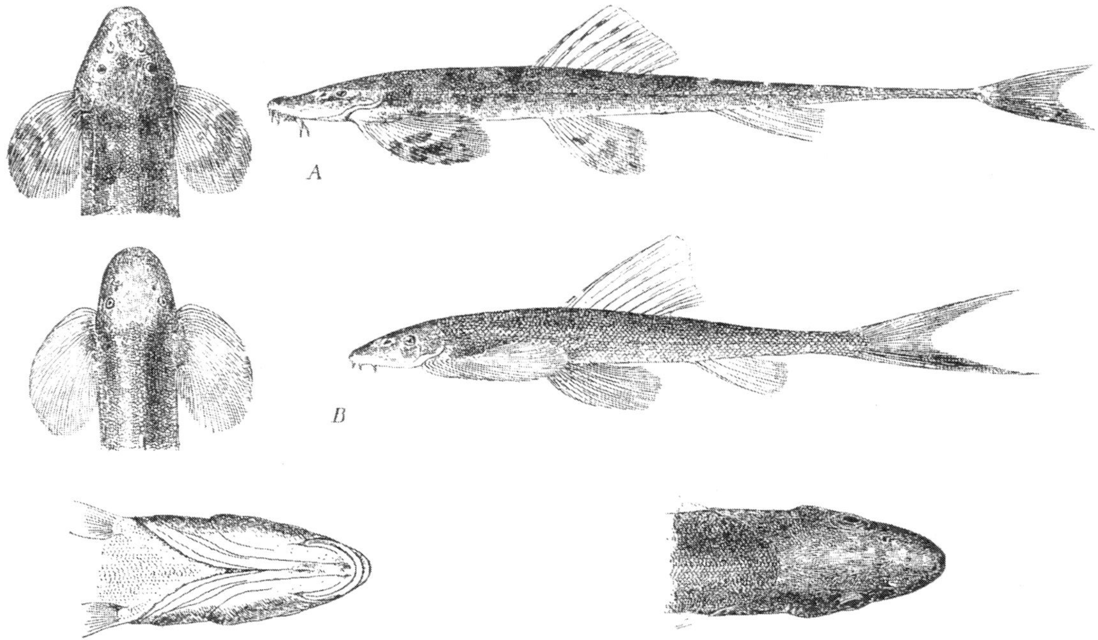

PLATE III.

39. *Misgurnus mizolepis*, sp. n. D. 7 or 8. A. 8, 9. V. 6 or 7.

This species has larger scales than any other of the genus known to me; they are arranged in thirteen longitudinal rows between the dorsal fin and the lateral line, and in ten between the lateral line and the ventral fin. Barbels ten, four belonging to the mandible; the inner pair of the mandibulary barbels are about half the length of the outer ones. Head and body compressed. The height of the body is nearly equal to the length of the head, which is contained six-and-a-half times in the total length (without caudal). Snout at least twice as long as the diameter of the eye, which is one-sixth of the length of the head. Origin of the dorsal fin nearer to the root of the caudal than to the occiput, conspicuously in advance of the root of the ventral fin. Pectoral fin a little shorter than the head; caudal fin rounded, continued by a series of rudimentary rays to the anal fin, and a similar distance forward on the dorsal edge of the tail; the rudimentary rays under the free portion of the tail are particularly deep. Greyish green, with a greyish line along each series of scales; lower parts whitish, finely mottled with brown.

Three specimens, of which the largest is 6½ inches long, from Kiu-kiang.

40. *Nemachilus xanthi*, sp. n. D. 12. A. 7. V. 8.

Scales minute but conspicuous. Caudal fin deeply emarginate; the origin of the dorsal fin is midway between the end of the snout and the root of the caudal. The height of the body is considerably less than the length of the head which is one-fourth of the total (without caudal). Snout of moderate length, pointed, as long as the postorbital portion of the head; eye of moderate size. A skinny adipose lobe occupies the place of the enlarged axillary scales of the pectoral and ventral fins. Back crossed by fourteen narrow brownish bands; a small black spot at the end of the lateral line; each caudal lobe with four oblique blackish bands each dorsal ray with one or two blackish specks.

One specimen, 4½ inches long, from Ichang.

41. *Nemachilus stoliczkæ* (Day). Kia-tiang-fu.

42. *Botia variegata*, sp. n. D. 11. A. 8. V. 9.

Barbels six. The height of the body is one-fifth of the total length (without caudal), the length of the head two-sevenths; snout elongate, but the small eye is much nearer to the end of the snout than to that of the operculum. The suborbital spine extends to below the hind margin of the orbit. Interorbital space narrow, transversely convex, twice as wide as the orbit. Origin of the dorsal fin midway between the root of the caudal and the orbit. Caudal fin deeply forked. Body covered with minute but regularly arranged scales. Ground colour yellowish, the body ornamented with five black bands, which are irregular in shape, and may be broken up into large blotches; all are continuous across the back, and the middle one corresponds in position to the dorsal fin. All the fins variegated with black, the black markings of the dorsal and anal fins sometimes confluent into broad band-like spots.

Two specimens of this fine gigantic species of loach were sent by Mr. Pratt from Ichang. The larger measures thirteen inches in length.

43. *Botia pratti*, sp. n. D. 11. A. 8. V. 9. (Plate IV. Fig. A.)

Barbels eight, but the two symphyseal barbels are not prolonged into filaments—more like a pair of soft round buttons. The height of the body is rather more than one-fifth of the total length (without caudal), the length of the head two-sevenths; snout elongate, but the very small eye is rather nearer to the end of the snout than to that of the operculum. The suborbital spine extends to below the hind margin of the orbit. Interorbital space narrow, transversely convex, three or four times as wide as the very small eye. Origin of the dorsal fin midway between the root of the caudal and the orbit. Caudal fin deeply forked, the lobes being as long as the head; body covered with minute but imbricate scales. Ground colour brownish olive, without distinct markings on the body. Dorsal fin with two blackish bands running parallel to the upper margin. Caudal rays with numerous linear black markings or without any spots; the lower fins with very indistinct blackish markings.

Three specimens eight inches long, from Kia-tiang-fu, 1,070 feet (foot of Omie-shan), Province Sze Chuen.

44. *Botia superciliaris*, sp. n. D. 11. A. 8. V. 8. (Plate IV. Fig. B.)

Barbels eight, but the two symphyseal barbels are not prolonged into filaments—more like a pair of soft round buttons. The height of the body is two-ninths of the total length (without caudal), the length of the head two-sevenths; snout elongate, the small eye being rather nearer to the end of the operculum than to that of the stout. The suborbital spine lies in a long cleft which extends beyond the eye in both directions. Interorbital space narrow, transversely convex, two-and-a-half times as wide as the eye. Origin of the dorsal fin midway between the root of the caudal and the eye. Caudal fin forked, the lobes being shorter than the head. Body covered with minute scales which are imbricate on the tail. Ground colour light olive with broad brownish bars across the back, five in front and five behind the dorsal fin. A yellowish streak on the side of the snout running backwards through the superciliary region; three yellowish longitudinal lines on the crown of the head. Dorsal and generally pectoral fin with a broad dark cross band well within the margin. Each caudal lobe with three or four dark oblique bands.

Five specimens six inches long, Kia-tiang-fu, 1,070 feet (foot of Omie-shan), Province Sze Chuen.

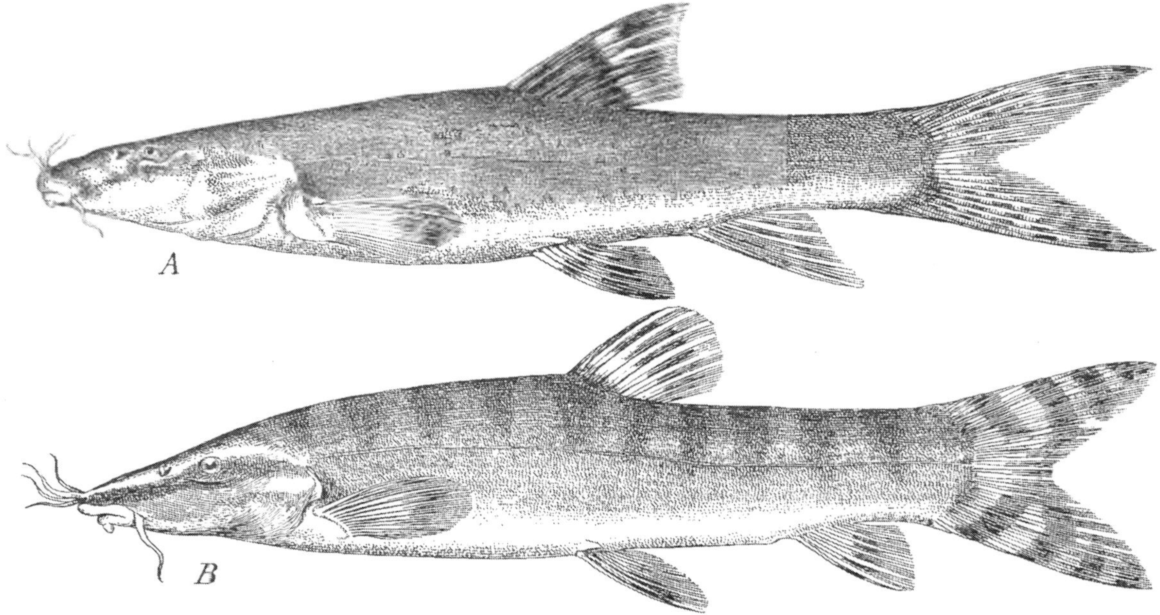

PLATE IV.

III

List of Lepidoptera collected by the author at Kiu-kiang. Extracts from a Paper by J. H. Leech, Esq., B.A., F.L.S. &c. Trans. Ent. Soc., Lond. March 1889.

1. *Euplœa midamus*, Linn.; Kirby, Cat. Diurn. Lep.
2. *Lethe butleri*, Leech, new species.
3. *Lethe naias*, Leech, n. s.
4. *Lethe syrcis*, Hew., Ex. Butt.; Oberth. Et. Ent.
5. *Neope ? muirheadii*, Feld., Wien. Ent. Mon.
   ? Debis segonax, Hew., Ex. Butt.
   Neope segonacia, Oberth. Et. Ent.
6. *Melanargia halimede*, Mén., Schrenk's Reise.
   Var *meridionalis*, Feld., Wien. Ent. Mon.
7. *Palæonympha opalina*, Butl., Trans. Ent. Soc. Lond. Lep. Exot.
8. *Satyrus dryas*, Scop., Ent. Carn.
   Satyrus bipunctatus, Motsch., Et. Ent.
   Var *sibirica*, Staud., Cat.
9. *Mycalesis regalis*, Leech, n. s.
10. *Mycalesis gotama*, Moore, Cat. Lep. E. I. C., Trans. Ent. Soc. Lond.
11. *Mycalesis perdiccas*, Hew. Ex. Butt.
    Mycalesis sangaica, Butl. Ann. & Mag. Nat. Hist.
12. *Ypthima motschulskyi*, Brem. & Grey, Schmett. Nordl. China's; Men., Cat. Mus. Petr.
13. *Ypthima sakra*, Moore, Cat. Lep. E. I. C., Hew., Trans. Ent. Soc. Lond.

14. *Ypthima baldus*, Fab. Syst. Ent.
Y. argus, Butl. Journ. Linn. Soc., Zool.
Y. zodia, Butl., Trans. Ent. Soc. Lond.
Y. evanescens, Butl. Ann. & Mag. Nat. Hist.

15. *Acræa vesta*, Fabr. Mant. Inst.; Don., Ins. China; Kirby, Cat. Diurn. Lep.

16. *Argynnis sagana*, Doubl., Gen.
Damora paulina, Nordm. Bull. Mosc.

17. *Argynnis paphia*, Linn.
♀ Var *valesina*, Esp.

18. *Argynnis laodice*, Pall., Reise.
Var *japonica*, Mén., Cat.

19. *Argynnis anadyomene*, Feld., Wien. Ent. Mon.
A. ella, Brem., Lep. Ost. Sib.

20. *Argynnis niphe*, Linn.

21. *Argynnis adippe*, Linn.; P. Z. S.

22. *Argynnis nerippe*, Feld., Wien. Ent. Mon.
A. coreana, Butl., Ann. & Mag. Nat. Hist.

23. *Melitæa maculata*, Br. & Grey, Schmett. Nordl. China's.
Argynnis leopardina, Lucas, Ann. Soc. Ent. de France.

24. *Vanessa c.-album*, Linn.; P. Z. S.

25. *Vanessa c.-aureum*, Linn.
V. angelica, Cram., Pap. Exot.

26. *Vanessa charonia*, Drury, Exot. Ent.; Brem., Lep. Ost. Sib.

27. *Parymeis indica*.
Papilio atalanta indica, Herbst.
Vanessa callirhoë, Fabr.

28. *Vanessa cardui*, Linn.

29. *Hestina assimilis*, Linn.

30. *Limenitis sydyi*, Led., Verh. Zool. Bot. Ges.

31. *Limenitis helmanni*, Led. Verh. Zool. Bot. Ges.

32. *Neptis aceris*, Lep., Reise.
Var *intermedia*, Pryer.

33. *Neptis eurynome*, West. Don., Inst. China.
Papilio leucothoë, Don., Inst. China.

34. *Neptis pryeri*, Butl., Trans. Ent. Soc. Lond.; Lep. Exot.; Jans., Cist. Ent.
Limenitis arboretum, Oberth., Et. Ent.

35. *Athyma sulpitia*, Cram., Pap. Exot.
Var *ningpoana*, Feld., Wien. Ent. Mon.

36. *Athyma fortuna*, Leech, n. s.

37. *Apatura ilia*, Schiff., S. V.
A. here, Feld., Wien. Ent. Mon.

38. *Apatura subalba*, Pouj., Ann. Soc. Ent. Fr.

39. *Charaxes narcæus*, Hew., Exot., Butt.
Var *mandarinus*, Feld., Reise Nov. Lep.

40. *Polyommatus phlæas*, Linn.
Var *chinensis*, Feld., Verh. Zool. Bot. Ges. Wien.
Var *eleus*, Fab.

41. *Lycæna argiades*, Pall.; Proc. Zool. Soc.

42. *Lycæna fischeri*, Eversm., Bull. Im.
L. davidi, Pouj., Ann. Soc. Fr.
L. filicaudis, Pryer.

43. *Lycæna argia*, Mén., Cat. Mus. Petr.
L. opalina, Pouj., Ann. Soc. Ent. Fr.

44. *Lycæna argiolus*, Linn.
L. ladonides, de l'Orza, Lep. Jap.
L. levetti, Butl. Ann. & Mag. Nat. Hist.

45. *Lycæna moorei*, Leech, n. s.

46. *Niphanda fusca*.

Thecla fusca, Brem. & Grey, Schmett. Nordl. China's; Proc. Zool. Soc.

47. *Thecla w. album*, var *eximia*, Fixsn.

48. *Thecla micans*, Brem. & Grey, Schmett. Nordl. China's.
T. betuloides, Blanch., Compt. Rend.

49. *Thecla pratti*, Leech, n. s.

50. *Curetis acuta*, Moore Ann. & Mag. Nat. Hist.

51. *Amblypodia rama*, Koll., Hug. Kaschm.; Hew., Cat. Lyc. B. M.
A. querceti, Moore, Cat. Lep. E. I. C.
♀ *A. dodonæa*, Moore, l. c.

52. *Amblypodia avidiena*, Hew., Ent. Mo. Mag.

53. *Terias læta*, Boisd., Sp. Gen.
Var *jægeri*, Mén., Cat. Mus. Petr.
T. subfervens, Butl., Ann. & Mag. Nat. Hist.

54. *Terias hecabe*, Linn., P. Z. S.

55. *Terias bethesba*, Janson, Cist. Ent.

56. *Pieris rapæ*, Linn.
P. crucivora, Boisd., Sp. Gén.
Var *orientalis*, Oberth., Et. Ent.

57. *Pieris canidia*, Sparrm.
P. gliciria, Cram., Pap. Exot.
P. clavipennis, Butl., Ann. & Mag. Nat. Hist.
P. sordida, Butl.

58. *Pieris napi*, Linn.
Var *melete*, Mén., Cat. Mus. Petr.

59. *Callidryas crocale*, Cram., Pap. Exot.
C. jugurtha, Cram., op. c.

60. *Rhodocera rhamni*, Linn.
R. nipalensis, Doubl. Gen. Diurn. Lep.
R. maxima, Butl., Trans. Ent. Soc. Lond.

61. *Colias hyale*, Linn., P. Z. S.

62. *Sericinus telamon*, Don., Ins. China, P. Z. S.

63. *Papilio elwesi*, Leech, n. s.

64. *Papilio aristolochiæ*, Fabr., Syst. Ent.

65\. *Papilio pamnon*, Linn.
Var *borealis*, Feld., Wien. Ent. Mon.

66\. *Papilio bianor*, Cram., Pap. Exot.; Lep. Jap. & Cor. P. Z. S.

67\. *Papilio demetrius*, Cram., Pap. Exot.
Var *carpenteri*, Butl., Ann. & Mag. Nat. Hist.

68\. *Papilio alcinous*, Klug., Neue Schmett.
P. alcinous, var. Gray, Cat. Lep. Ins.
P. mencius, Feld., Wien. Ent. Mon.
P. spathatus, Butl., Ann. & Mag. Nat. Hist.
P. plutonius, Oberth., Et. Ent.

69\. *Papilio sarpedon*, L., var.

70\. *Papilio xuthus*, Linn.
Var *xuthulus*, Brem., Lep. Ost. Sib.

71\. *Papilio machaon*, Linn.
Var *asiatica*, Mén., Enum.
Var *hippocrates*, Feld, Verh. Zool.-bot. Ges. Wien.

72\. *Papilio macilentus*, Janson, Cist. Ent.
Papilio tractipennis, Butl., Ann. & Mag., Nat. Hist.
P. scævola, Oberth., Et. Ent.

73\. *Ismene badra*, Moore, Cat. Lep. E.I.C.

74\. *Pamphila mathias*, Fabr., Ent. Syst. Suppl.

75\. *Pamphila oceia*, Hew., Desc. Hesp.

76\. *Pamphila guttata*, Murr., P.Z.S.
Eudamus guttatus, Brem. & Grey, Schmett. Nordl. China's.
Goniloba guttata, Mén., Cat. Mus. Petr.

77\. *Pamphila fortunei*, Feld., Reise Nov.

78\. *Pamphila prominens*, Moore.
Gegenes sinensis, Mab., Bull. Soc. Zool. Fr.

79\. *Pamphila mencia*, Moore, Ann. & Mag. Nat. Hist.

80\. *Gegenes hainanus*, Moore, P.Z.S.

81\. *Hesperia sylvatica*, Brem., Lep. Ost. Sib.

82\. *Syricthus maculatus*, Brem. & Grey, Schmett. Nordl. China's.

83. *Plesioneura bifasciata.*
Eudamus bifasciatus, Brem. & Grey, Schmett. Nordl. China's.
Gonilobia bifasciata, Mén., Cat. Mus. Petr.

84. *Tagiades nymphealis*, Speyer, Stett. Ent. Zeit.

85. *Pterygospidea maculosa*, Feld., Reise Nov.

86. *Pterygospidea sinica*, Feld., Wien. Ent. Mon.
Pterygospidea moorei, Mab., Bull. Soc. Ent. France.
Daimio felderi, Butl. Ann. & Mag. Nat. Hist.

87. *Pterygospidea davidii*, Mab., Bull. Soc. Ent. France.

88. *Antigonus vasava*, Moore, P.Z.S.

89. *Acherontia atropos*, Linn.
Acherontia styx, Westw., Cab. Orient. Ent.
Acherontia medusa, Butl., Trans. Zool. Soc.; Ill. Typ. Lep. Het.

90. *Acherontia morta*, Hübn., Verz. Schmett.
Acherontia atropos, var. Cram., Pap. Exot.
A. lethe, Westw., Cab. Orient. Ent.
A satanas, Boisd., Nat. Hist. Lep.

91. *Smerinthus ocellatus*, Linn.
Smerinthus planus, Walk., Cat. Lep. Het.
S. argus, Mén., Cat. Mus. Petr.

92. *Smerinthus dissimilis*, Brem., Lep. Ost. Sib.

93. *Ampelophaga rubiginosa*, Brem. & Grey, Beitr. zur Schmett. Faun. Nord. China.

94. *Clanis bilineata*, Walk., Cat. Lep. Het. Suppl.; Butl., Ill. Typ. Lep. Het.

95. *Acosmeryx anceus*, Cram., Pap. Exot.

96. *Daphnusa colligata*, Walk., Cat. Lep. Het.
Metagastes bietii, Oberth., Lep. du Tibet.

97. *Lophura sangaica*, Butl., P.Z.S.

98. *Diludia increta*, Walk., Cat. Lep. Het.; Butl., Ill. Typ. Lep. Het.

99. *Chærocampa japonica*, Bois., Ins. Lep. Het.

100. *Chærocampa silhetensis*, Walk., Cat. Lep. Het.; Butl., Ill. Typ. Lep. Het.
Chærocampa bisecta, Moore, cf. Butl. l. c.

101. *Chærocampa elpenor*, Linn.
Chærocampa lewisii, Butl., Proc. Zool. Soc.

102. *Pergesa mongoliana*, Butl., Proc. Zool. Soc.; Ill. Typ. Lep. Het.

103. *Leucophlebia lineata*, Westw., Cab. Orient. Ent.

104. *Macroglossa pyrrhosticta*, Butl., Proc. Zool. Soc.

105. *Macroglossa bombylans*, Boisd., Ins. Lep. Het.

106. *Sataspes infernalis*, Westw., Cab. Orient. Ent.

107. *Hemaris radians*, Walk., Cat. Lep. Het.; Butl. Ill. Typ. Lep. Het.

108. *Sciapteron chinense*, Leech, n. s.
HYPERTHYRUS, Leech, n. g.

109. *Hyperthyrus aperta*, Leech, n. s.

110. *Eusemia japana*
Chelonomorpha japana, Motsch., Etud. Ent.
Eusemia villicoides, Butl., Ann. & Mag. Nat. Hist.

111. *Seudyra subflava*, Moore, Ann. & Mag. Nat. Hist.

112. *Retina costata*, Walk., Cat. Lep. Het; Butl., Ill. Typ. Lep. Het.

113. *Eterusia ædea*, Clerck, Icon.

114. *Soritia elizabetha*, Walk., Cat. Lep. Het.

115. *Histia flabellicornis*, Fabr., Sp. Ins.; Walk., Cat. Lep. Het.

116. *Epicopeia mencia*, Moore, Proc. Zool. Soc.

117. *Arachotia hyalina*, Leech, n. s.

118. *Phauda fortuneii*, H. S., Lep. Exot. Sp. Nov.
Phauda triadum, Walk., Cat. Lep. Het.

119. *Syntomis muirheadii*, Feld., Wien. Ent. Mon.

120. *Syntomis pratti*, Leech, n. s.

121. *Syntomis pascus*, Leech, n. s.

122. *Syntomis thelebus*, Fabr.
Syntomis germana, Feld., Wien. Ent. Mon.
S. mandarinia, Butl., J. L. S., Zool.

123. *Syntomis torquatus*, Leech, n. s.

124. *Alpenus flammeolus*, Moore, Ann. & Mag. Nat. Hist.

125. *Rhodogastria lactinea*, Cram., Pap. Exot.
R. sanguinolenta, Fabr., Ent. Syst.

126. *Dionychopus niveus*, Mén., Bull. Phys. Petersb.

127. *Rhyparioides rubescens*, Walk., Cat. Lep. Het.
var. *amurensis*, Brem., Lep. Ost-Sib.

128. *Diacrisia subvaria*, Walk., Cat. Lep. Het.; Butl., Ill. Typ. Lep. Het.

129. *Cystidia stratonice*, Cram., Pap. Exot.
Vithora agrionides, Butl., Ann. & Mag. Nat. His.; Ill. Typ. Lep. Het.

130. *Hypercompa principalis*, Kollar, var. *regalis*.

131. *Trypheromera plagifera*, Walk., Cat. Lep. Het.

132. *Bizone sanguinea*, Brem., Schmett. Nordl. China's.

133. *Bizone hamata*, Walk., Cat. Lep. Het.

134. *Bizone phædra*, Leech, n. s.

135. *Hypoprepia delineata*, Walk., Cat. Lep. Het.

136. *Digama abietis*, Leech, n. s.

137. *Eligma narcissus*, Cram., Pap. Exot.

138. *Lithosia vetusta*, Walk., Cat. Lep. Het.

139. *Numenes disparilis*, Staud., Rom. Mem. sur les Lép.

140. *Laria l-nigrum*, Muller, Faun. Fr.

141. *Porthetria dispar*, Linn.
Liparis dispar, var *japonica*, Motsch., Etud. Ent.
Porthetria umbrosa, Butl., Trans. Ent. Soc. Lond.
P. hadina, Butl., l. c.

142. *Leucoma salicis*, Linn.

143. *Belippa horrida*, Walk., Cat. Lep. Het.

144. *Attacus cynthia*, Drury, App.; Cram. Pap. Exot.
Attacus pryeri, Butl., Proc. Zool. Soc.; Ill. Typ. Lep. Het.
A. walkeri, Feld., Wien. Ent. Mon.

145. *Actias sinensis*, Walk., Cat. Lep. Het.

146. *Actias selene*, Hübn., Verz. Schmett.
A. ningpoana, Feld.
Tropœa artemis, Brem., Etud. Entom. de Motschulsky; Lep. Ost-Sib.
T. gnoma, Butl., Ann. & Mag. Nat. Hist.; Ill. Typ. Lep. Het.

147. *Antherœa pernyi*, Guerin, Rev. et Mag. Zool.
A. hazina, Butl., Trans. Ent. Soc. Lond.

147*a*. *Saturnia pyretorum*, Boisduval MSS.; Westw., Cab. Orient. Ent.

148. *Brahmœa undulata*, Brem., Schmett. Nordl. China's.

149. *Clisiocampa neustria*, Linn.

150. *Odonestis læta*, Walk., Cat. Lep. Het.

151. *Trabala vishnu*, Lef., Zoòl. Journ.
var. *sulphurea*, Kollar, Kaschmir, Von Hugel.
T. basalis, Walk., Lep. Het.

152. *Phassus sinensis*, Moore, Ann. & Mag. Nat. Hist.

153. *Thyatira trimaculata*, Brem., Bull. Acad. Sci. St. Pet.; Lep. Ost-Sib.

154. *Acronycta rumicis*, Linn.

155. *Moma* (*Noctua*) *orion*, Esp., Tr., Dup., Frr. B., Guén.
Noctua aprilina, Wien. Verz.; Fabr., Mant. Inst.; Hübn., Eur. Schmett. Noct.
Diphtera orion, Walk., Cat. Lep. Het.

156. *Mythimna turca*, Linn.

157. *Mythimna placida*, Butl., Ann. & Mag. Nat. Hist.; Ill. Typ. Lep. Het.

158. *Mythimna* (*Leucania*) *singularis*, Butl., Ann. & Mag. Nat. Hist.; Ill. Typ. Lep. Het.
M. formosana, Butl., P. Z. S.

159. *Leucania decisissima*, Walk., Cat. Lep. Het.
L. salebrosa, Butl., Ann. & Mag. Nat. Hist.; Ill. Typ. Lep. Het.
L. rufistrigosa, Moore, P. Z. S.

160. *Leucania extranea*, Guen., Noct.

161. *Leucania simplex*, Leech, n. s.

162. *Cloantha polyodon*, Clerck.
C. perspicillaris, Linn.
C. orontii, Her.-Schaff., Schmett. Eur.
C. intermedia, Brem., Bull. de l'Acad.; Lep. Ost-Sib.

163. *Mamestra thoracica*, Walk., Cat. Lep. Het.

164. *Mamestra dolorosa*, Walk., Cat. Lep. Het.

165. *Perigea illecta*, Walk., Cat. Lep. Het.

166. *Hadena funerea*, Hein., Schm. D.
Xylophasia sodalis, Butl., Ann. & Mag. Nat. Hist.; Ill. Typ. Lep. Het.

167. *Caradrina cæca*, Oberth., Diag. Lep. Ask.

168. *Hermonassa cecilia*, Butl., Ann. & Mag. Nat. Hist.; Ill. Typ. Lep. Het.

169. *Agrotis ypsilon*, Rott., Naturf.
A. suffusa, Hübn.

170. *Graphiphora dahlii*, Hübn.
G. canescens, Butl., Ann. & Mag. Nat. Hist.; Ill. Typ. Lep. Het.

171. *Graphiphora brunnea*, Fabr.

172. *Graphiphora pacifica*, Butl., Ann. & Mag. Nat. Hist.; Ill. Typ. Lep. Het.

173. *Aplectoides caligenea*, Butl., Trans. Ent. Soc. Lond.

174. *Polydesma vulgaris*, Butl., P. Z. S.

175. *Eurois exclusa*, Leech, n. s.

176. *Penicillaria geyeri*, Feld., Reise der Nov.

177. *Callopistria purpureofasciata*, Piller.
C. pteridis, Fabr., Ent. Syst.
C. exotica, Guen., Noct.
C. duplicans, Walk., Cat. Lep. Het.

178. *Acontia bicolora*, Leech, n. s.

179. *Hecatera fasciata*, Leech, n. s.

180. *Dianthœcia compta*, Fabr., Mant.

181. *Plusia albostriata*, Brem. & Grey, Beitr. zur Schmett. Fauna des Nordl. China.

182. *Plusiodonta compressipalpis*, Guen., Noct.

183. *Gonitis mesogona*, Walk., Cat. Lep. Het.

184. *Gonitis albitibia*, Walk., Cat. Lep. Het.

185. *Amphipyra pyramidea*, Linn.
A. monolitha, Guen., Noct.; Walk., Cat. Lep. Het.
A. magna, Walk., Cat. Lep. Het. Suppl.
var *obscura*, Oberth., Etud. Entom.

186. *Amphipyra livida*, Fabr., Mant.
A. corvina, Motsch., Bull. Soc. Mosc.

187. *Nænia contaminata*.
Graphiphora contaminata, Walk., Cat. Lep. Het. Suppl.

188. *Mormo muciviren*s, Butl., Ann. & Mag. Nat. Hist.; Ill. Typ. Lep. Het.

189. *Orthogonia sera*, Feld., Wien. Ent. Mon.
Orthogonia crispina, Butl., Ann. & Mag. Nat. Hist.; Ill. Typ. Lep. Het.

190. *Dichonia bipunctata*, Motsch., Etud. Ent.

191. *Toxocampa lilacina*, Butl., Ann. & Mag. Nat. Hist.; Ill. Typ Lep. Het.

T. recta, Brem.

192. *Calpe excavata*, Butl., Ann. & Mag. Nat. Hist.; Ill. Typ. Lep. Het.

193. *Lacera procellosa*, Butl., Ann. & Mag. Nat. Hist.

194. *Sypna achatina*, Butl., Cist. Ent.; Ill. Typ. Lep. Het.

195. *Sypna astrigera*, Butl., Cist. Ent.

196. *Sypna distincta*, Leech, n. s.

197. *Ophideres tyrannus*, Guen., Noct.

198. *Ophideres fullonica*, Linn.

199. *Ophideres salaminia*, Cram., Pap. Exot.

200. *Lagoptera dotata*, Fabr.

201. *Lagoptera elegans*, Van der Hoven, Lep. Nov.

202. *Catocala esther*, Butl., Cist. Ent.; Ill. Typ. Lep. Het.
C. numægeni, Staud.

203. *Catocala volcanica*, Butl., Cist. Ent.; Ill. Typ. Lep. Het.

204. *Chrysorithrum amatum*, Brem., Ménétriés, Cat. Lep. Mus. Petrop.

205. *Patula macrops*, Linn.
P. boopis, Guen. Noct.

206. *Nyctipao crepuscularis*, Linn.

207. *Spiramia retorta*, ♀, Linn., Mus. Lud. Ulr.; Cram., Pap. Exot.
S. retorta, ♂, Cram., Pap. Exot.; *suffumosa*, Guen. Noct.
S. spiralis, Fabr., Sp. Ins.
S. japonica, Guen., Noct.
S. jinchuena, Butl., Ann. & Mag. Nat. Hist.
S. inæqualis, Butl., l. c.

208. *Spiramia martha*, Butl., Ann. & Mag. Nat. Hist.; Ill. Typ. Lep. Het.
S. agrota, Butl., Trans. Ent. Soc. Lond.

209. *Calliodes rectifasciata*, Henety.
Spiramia interlineata, Butl., Ann. & Mag. Nat. Hist.; Ill. Typ. Lep. Het.

210. *Cocytodes modesta*, Van der Hoven, Lep. Nouv.

211. *Ophiusa falcata*, Moore., Descr. Ind. Lep. Atk.

212. *Ophiusa algira*, Linn.
O. stuposa, Fabr., Ent. Syst.

213. *Ophiusa arctotænia*, Guen., Noct.; Walk., Cat. Lep. Het.

214. *Grammodes mygdon*, Cram., Pap. Exot.

215. *Remigia archesia*, Cram., Pap. Exot.
R. virbia, Cram., l. c.

216. *Remigia annetta*, Butl., Ann. & Mag. Nat. Hist.; Ill. Typ. Lep. Het.

217. *Sonagara vialis*, Moore, P. Z. S.

218. *Ophiodes triphænoides*, Walk., Cat. Lep. Het.
O. cuprea, Moore, P. Z. S.

219. *Ophiodes tirrhæa*, Cram., Pap. Exot.
O. vesta, Esp., Schmett.
O. olivacea, Vill., Ent. Linn.
O. auricularis, Hübn., Noct.
O. hottentota, Guen., Noct.
O. separans, Walk., Cat. Lep. Het.

220. *Serrodes campana*, Guen., Noct.

221. *Ophisma gravata*, Guen., Noct.

222. *Potamorphora manlia*, Cram., Pap. Exot.

223. *Hulodes caranea*, Cram., Pap. Exot.

224. *Urapteryx delectans*, Butl., Ill. Typ. Lep. Het.

225. *Odontoptera mandarinata*, Leech, n. s.

226. *Geometra viridiluteata*, Walk., Cat. Lep. Het.

227. *Thalera strigata*, Muel., Faun. Ins. Fr.
T. (Hemithea) thymiaria, Guen., Phal.

228. *Thalera crenulata*, Butl., Ann. & Mag. Nat. Hist.; Ill. Typ. Lep. Het.

229. *Ephyra grata*, Butl., Ann. & Mag. Nat. Hist.

230. *Bizia æxaria*, Walk., Cat. Lep. Het.; Butl., Ill. Typ. Lep. Het.
Eudropia mibuaria, Feld., Reise der Nov., Lep.

231. *Elphos latiferaria*, Walk., Lep. Het.; Butl., Ill. Typ. Lep. Het.

232. *Boarmia picata*, Butl., Trans. Ent. Soc. Lond.

233. *Boarmia consortaria*, Fabr.
B. conferenda, Butl., Ann. & Mag. Nat. Hist.

234. *Boarmia grisea*, Butl., Ann. & Mag. Nat. Hist.; Ill. Typ. Lep. Het.

235. *Boarmia ocellata*, Leech, n. s.

236. *Stenotrachelys cinerea*, Butl., Trans. Ent. Soc. Lond.

237. *Buzura abraxata*, Leech, n. s.

238. *Pachyodes arenaria*, Leech, n. s.

239. *Rhyparia jaguaria*, Guen., Phal.

240. *Abraxas sylvata*, Scop., Ent. Carn.
A. ulmata, Fabr., Syst. Ent.
A. miranda, Butl., Ann. & Mag. Nat. Hist.; Ill. Typ. Lep Het.

241. *Abraxas martaria*, Guen., Phal.

242. *Abraxas junctilineata*, Walk., Cat. Lep. Het.; Butl., Ill. Typ. Lep. Het.

243. *Abraxas amplificata*, Walk., Cat. Lep. Het.

243a. *Abraxas interruptaria*, Feld., Wien. Ent. Mon.; Reise der Nov.

244. *Panæthia hemionata*, Guen., Phal.

245. *Obeida vagipardata*, Walk., Cat. Lep. Het.

246. *Aspilates mundataria*, Cram., Pap. Exot.
A. tonghata, Feld., Reise der Nov.

247. *Percnia foraria*, Guen., Phal.

248. *Acidalia strigilaria*, Hübn.
A. vagata, Walk., Cat. Lep. Het.

249. *Acidalia indicataria.*
Argyris indicataria, Walk., Cat. Lep. Het.; Butl., Ill. Typ. Lep. Het.

250. *Asthena superior*, Butl., Ann. & Mag. Nat. Hist.; Ill. Typ. Lep. Het.

251. *Timandra amataria*, Linn.
T. comptaria, Walk., Cat. Lep. Het.; Butl., Ill. Typ. Lep. Het.

252. *Macaria zachera*, Butl., Ann. & Mag. Nat. Hist.; Ill. Typ. Lep. Het.

253. *Macaria sinicaria*, Walk., Cat. Lep. Het.
M. proditaria, Brem., Lep. Ost-Sib.
M. maligna, Butl., Ann. & Mag. Nat. Hist.; Ill. Typ. Lep. Het.

254. *Carige duplicaria*, Walk., Cat. Lep. Het.
Macaria nigronotaria, Brem., Lep. Ost-Sib.

255. *Melanippe procellata*, Hübn.
M. inquinata, Butl., Ann. & Mag. Nat. Hist.; Ill. Typ. Lep. Het.

256. *Melanippe ? undulata*, Leech, n. s.

257. *Micronia pontiata*, Guen., Phal.; Walk., Cat. Lep. Het.

258. *Cidaria macatata*, Feld., Reise der Nov.

New Species and Varieties of Lepidoptera collected by the Author in Western and Central China, described and named by J. H. Leech, Esq., B.A., F.L.S., etc., in the 'Entomologist,' 1890 *and* 1891.

FEBRUARY 1890

Zethera sagitta.
Melanargia halimede.
var. montana.
Lethe cyrene.
" occulta.
" trimacula.
" nigrifascia.
" labyrinthea.
Neope ramosa.
" romanovi.
Satyrus maculosa.
Pararge catena.
Callerebia albipuncta.
Clerome ærope.
Hestina nigrivena.
" viridis.
" oberthuri.
Euripus japonicus.
var. chinensis.
Apatura fasciola.
Athyma punctata.
" disjuncta.
" fortuna.
var. diffusa.
Limenitis pratti.
Neptis hesione.
" thisbe.
var. themis.
var. thetis.
" antilope.
Neptis cydippe.
" beroe.
" aspasia.
" antigone.
" arachne.
Iolaus luculentus.
" contractus.
Thecla elwesi.
" ornata.
" rubicundula.
Dipsas minerva.
" comes.
" melpomene.
" thespis.
Rapala repercussa.
" subpurpurea.
Lycæna arcana.
" nebulosa.
Satsuma chalybeia.
" pratti.
Amblypodia angulata.
" ganessa.
var. seminigra.
Dodona maculosa.
Leucophasia gigantea.
Pieris oberthuri.
Delias patrua.
Pterogospidea diversa.
Plesioneura grandis.
Pamphila virgata.

Pamphila maga.
„ similis.
Halpe submacula.
Cyclopides chinensis.
Cyclopides nanus.
Bizone cruenta.
♂ Saturnia oberthuri.

April 1890

Campylotes pratti.
Eusemia vithoroides.
Seudyra subalba.
„ mandarina.
„ flavida.
Chelonia bieti.
var. pratti.
Dionychopus rubidus.
Crinola flavicollis.
Gynæphora pluto.
Artaxa montis.
Orgyia prisca.
Numenes disparilis.
var. separata.
Jana mandarina.
Antheræa thespis.
Drepana parvula.
„ acuminata.
„ bidens
„ flavilinea.
Thyatira trimaculata.
var. chinensis.
var. albomaculata.

June 1890

Erebia ruricola.
„ rurigena.
Pararge præusta.
Argynnis zenobia.
Grapta gigantea.
Helcyra superba.
♀ Sephisa princeps.
Apatura pallas.
Thecla cœlestis.
Aporia procris.
Pieris lotis.
„ cisseis.
Papilio sciron.

January 1891

Zophoessa argentata.
„ helle.
„ procne.
„ libitina.
Lethe procris.
„ baucis.
„ helena.
„ hecate.
Lethe camilla.
Ypthima ciris.
Euthalia pratti.
„ staudingeri.
Euthalia hebe.
Pieris eurydice.
Urapteryx nigrociliaris.
„ parallelaria.

FEBRUARY 1891

Lethe simulans.
„ calisto.
„ gemina.
Neope oberthuri.
Neorina patria.
Ragadia latifasciata.
Acrophthalmia thalia.
Enispe lunatus.
Vanessa fenestra.
Hestina subviridis.
Euripus funebris.
Limenitis livida.
„ albomaculata.
Abrota pratti.
Euthalia consobrina.
„ omeia.
Apatura subcærulea.
„ fulva.
Charaxes ganymedes.
„ posidonius.

JUNE 1891

Ypthima iris.
Callerebia phyllis.
Melanargia leda.
♀ Pieris davidis (Oberth., Stud. Entom.).
„ davidis.
var. venata.
Thecla patrius.
Lycæna ion.
Eudamus simplex.
Eudamus proximus.
Syrichthus oberthuri.
Pamphila pulchra.
Carterocephalus gemmatus.
Taractrocera trimaculata.
„ lyde.
Nisoniades pelias.
Celænorrhinus consanguinea.
„ aspersa.

SEPTEMBER 1891

Neope simulans.
Ypthima insolita.
„ prænubila.
„ conjuncta.
Lethe laodamia.
Lethe titania.
„ christophi.
Neope (Satyrus) armandii.
var. fusca.

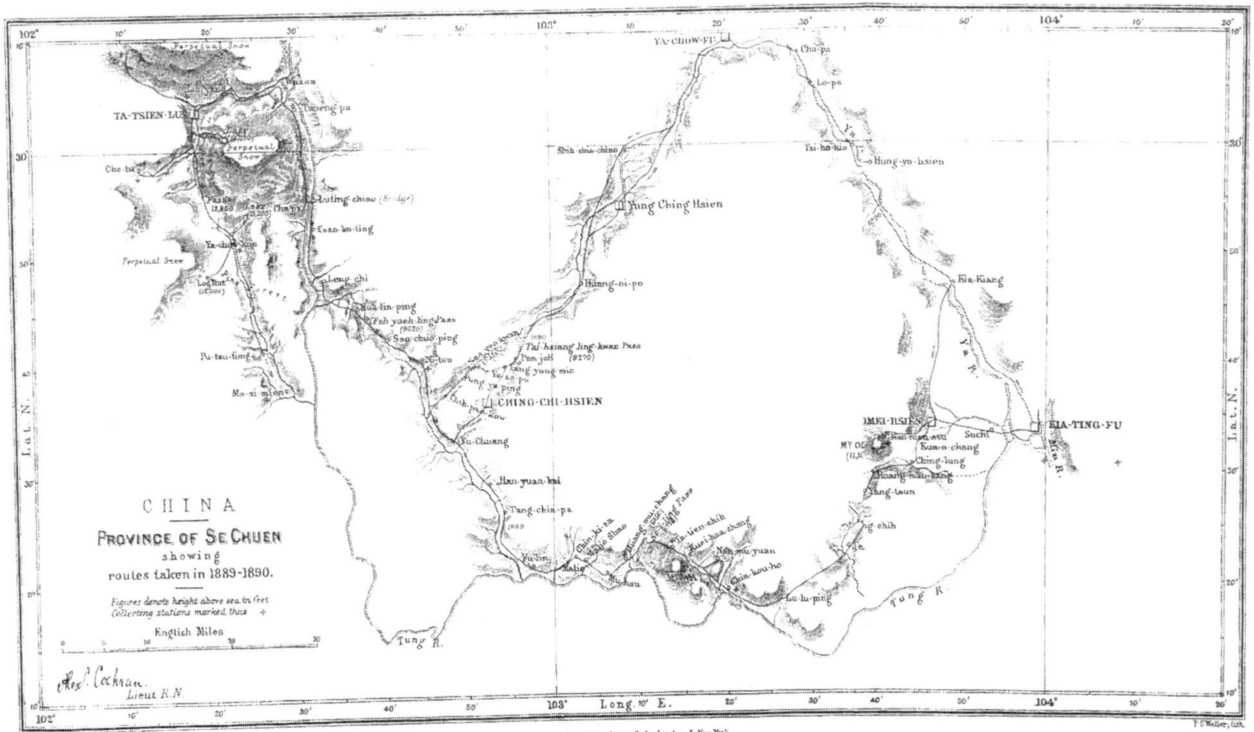
CHINA
PROVINCE OF SE CHUEN
showing
routes taken in 1889-1890.
Figures denote height above sea in feet
Collecting stations marked thus +
English Miles
Alex. Cochran.
Lieut. R.N.
TA-TSIEN-LU
YA-CHOW-FU
Yung Ching Hsien
CHING-CHI-HSIEN
KIA-TING-FU
Perpetual Snow
Luting-chiao (Bridge)
Tsao-ko-ting
Leng-chi
Hua-lin-ping
Feh yueh ling Pass
San-chiao-ping
Pu-tsu-fung
Mo-si-mien
Che-tung
Hiang-ni-po
Shih-chia-chiao
Tai-hsiang ling-kwan Pass
Fu-Chuang
Han-yuan-kai
Tang-chia-pa
Fu-lin
Chin-kou-ho
Lu-lu-ping
Tung R.
Ya R.
Min R.
Cha-pa
Lo-pa
Hung-ya-hsien
Kia-Kiang
Suchi
Kuo-o-chang
Ching-lung
Yang-tsun
Long. E.
Lat. N.
102°
103°
104°
30'
Longmans, Green & Co; London & New York.